Fell's Complete Guide
To Buried Treasure,
Land and Sea

Other Books on Treasure by the Author

Fell's Complete Guide
To Buried Treasure, Land and Sea

by

Lieut. Harry E. Rieseberg

6993

A World of Books That Fill a Need

Frederick Fell, Inc.   **New York**

Preface

ADVENTUROUS AND COURAGEOUS MEN have gone to the frozen poles, into the tropical wilds and burning deserts in their quest for knowledge. Others have traced ancient culture, establishing piece by piece the earliest dawn of civilization in the interest of scientific advancement. Thus, the earth has today been almost completely explored and the white spots on the maps which heretofore marked unexplored territory have gradually vanished until there are few remaining.

However, there still exists one field of exploration that has not as yet been conquered. The greatest field of all lingers —a new field that might be designated as mercenary or self-indulgent—the category of fortune-hunting with its adventures and thrills.

Down through the years, pirates, buccaneers, bandits, and early explorers, followed by New World prospectors of new lands, have left fabulous treasures in ill-fated shipwrecks and unnumbered mining camps of the past. From such discoveries many have made huge fortunes.

Few books have adequately described these lost sites of the lost ships which never made their ports or those lost and abandoned mines in which still rest fabulous riches beyond fancy's wildest dreams. They literally carpet the floor of the oceans and the earth's land surfaces.

The search for both sunken and buried treasure has
today become a new field of endeavor, one which is fast
becoming a universal lure for the modern age of sea and
land exploration. It is *real* and often most rewarding for all.
However, the general public usually thinks of these lost
treasures as something only fools put their faith in and arm-
chair dreamers read about, while adventurers seek it! But
they are in error, for there is more gold, silver, and other
wealth lying on the bottoms of seas, rivers, and lakes, and
resting in lost and abandoned mine sites than there is in the
combined treasuries of the countries of the world (omitting
foreign aid and defense spending). In fact, more wealth has
been extracted from out of long-disintegrated sunken shipwrecks and unearthed from lost and abandoned mining camp
sites during the past decade than has been spent in twenty-
five years of our government's actual cash budget!

I know, for I have partaken of some of the riches myself
during my many years engaged in actual treasure-hunting.

Today, those contemplating an underwater search do not
need colorful "so-called" treasure maps to pin-point the sites
where these more modern sunken argosies still rest, or where,
in the past, those of earlier vintage met their final anchorage.
True, there are those who advertise in various mediums the
sale of such maps and charts purporting to show the exact
location of sunken treasure shipwrecks, buried mining camps,
and other like spots. But those credulous unsuspecting enthusiasts who purchase such maps are easily deceived, and
they usually discover that their purchase is of little use, if
any at all. In this field one need only have knowledge of
diving and equipment, patience, a little luck, and the recorded place of the craft's sinking. Those who seek the sites
of lost and abandoned mines may find their locations only

through research and the use of electronic metal detectors.

During the past thirty years, I personally have compiled and brought together through substantiated research and, on various occasions, actual salvage investigations—from original source marine documents and records—some 300,000 dead files of lost ships which were formerly under my direction as a chief in the United States Bureau of Navigation and Steamboat Inspection Service. This is a precise catalog of known projects which would keep hundreds of earnest treasure-hunters busy for several lifetimes. And the further I have penetrated into this most fascinating research, together with that of my own business of treasure search and salvage for so many years, the more I have come to realize I have so far merely scratched the surface of the thousands of treasure-bearing craft which have been lost throughout the centuries in the world's seas, lakes, and rivers, and which still rest on the very spots where they went down.

To me, there is tragic drama in the history of each of these ill-fated ships, which still shelter their rich cargoes of incalculable wealth, decades or centuries after disaster had overwhelmed them. Even the mere names of these craft in my Catalog of Lost Treasure Ships produces flashing scenes in my mind—undersea waters burst into violent life.

I have had some success in my years of salvage operations, even brought to the surface on numerous occasions rich prizes in both treasure, relics, and artifacts of great value; sometimes great quantities of golden ingots, silver bars, sows and copper pigs, pieces of eight, doubloons and other rich finds. My salvage operations have been accomplished without prior publicity. So many treasure-hunters seem to immediately send releases to the press, but this is to their disadvantage. Even today, if I were much younger,

I have such complete confidence in my long years of labori-
ously garnered data, as well as my former salvaging ability,
I should like nothing better than to start out again on the
herculean schedule and task of finding them all!

I fully realize that such a stupendous feat is out of the
question—an impossibility at any time for a treasure salvor.
My days of actual treasure-hunting are now about over; I
have had my share of adventure and fortune in this field, and
must leave this work to the modern-day seeker of these
sunken finds. It is all quite clear, vivid, tremendously exciting
—and so often most profitable. It has been a thrilling experi-
ence, and imagination alone can never erase the craving from
a man's mind and heart once he has experienced the thrill
of having followed the adventurous calling of treasure salvage as a career.

Just as thrilling and exciting is that of searching for—
and finding on so many occasions—so many of the lost and
abandoned sites of the early mining camps and abandoned
diggings, which had so much to do with the making of early
American settlements, and from which stupendous fortunes
were derived. I owe most of the authenticated data on these
sites to my late friend Frank L. Fish, noted treasure-hunter
in this field, who, before his recent death, furnished me with
so much of the information incorporated herein as to the
clues and exact locations of these fabulous still-remaining
camps.

But for you who are anxious to go treasure-hunting—
either for sunken or buried riches—not that of some vague
fiction-writer's imagination, or some "purported" true site a
map-seller sells you—here, then, is a brand new kind of treasure handbook. These are not the tales of traditional and
fictitious treasures and pirates' gold which may or may not

have existed, but a true catalog of *actual* resting places of *real* treasure which still, even to this day, awaits recovery. All this waiting for the modern-day treasure-hunter. . . . *Good treasure searching!!*

(Lieut.) Harry E. Rieseberg

Contents

Fell's Complete Guide

To Buried Treasure,
Land and Sea

The Lure

of Sunken Treasure

BILLIONS OF DOLLARS in the shape of golden ingots, silver bars, precious jewels, and other treasure lie on the bottoms of the oceans, rivers, and lakes still awaiting modern-day salvage. Huge fortunes have been gained on untold successful recovery enterprises—and, too, many the fortunes lost. But the lure for riches still goes on as from time memorial.

The yellow and white metals! Glistening gems and jewels galore! The very words flame up a dazzling light in man's mind; the heart begins to beat more quickly, the nerves tingle. Gold! Silver! Ingots, nuggets, doubloons, ducats, pesos, pieces-of-eight—all crowd the vision, glittering in piles on the floors of the waters of the world, bursting in metallic cascades from newly discovered treasure-chests. What pots of riches there must be in the world, and the myriads of human beings who have, down through the centuries, searched for it, used it, abused it—even died for it! The lure of treasure-trove! How irresistible and how fatal! Where and how did the craving for wealth begin?

15

Let us turn back the pages of time and envision when the world first gave it thought, perhaps when Kalsah, in her golden leopard skin, danced before her master in those far-off days of primitive man. How it gleamed! Then, later, Egyptian and Jew, each in their golden arrogance, flit by like fading shadows; stealthy Phoenicians, in their crude white-sailed craft, laden with treasures from mysterious lands of the Old World, skim past; and still later, came the fabulous King Solomon's Mines! Then his temple at Jerusalem—that sacred temple of the Jewish nation—through its lure and craving for wealth, soon yielded its treasure-hoard of gold, and under the proud eagles of ancient Rome the winged cherubims crashed downward in the universal ruin and brought destruction upon the holy temple.

And so, as Jerusalem fell, in turn fell proud and arrogant Rome before the hosts of Gaul; and, as empire after empire grew rich, amassing untold riches and acquired habits of luxury and decadence, so the lure of treasure began and the conquerors to the spoil. Then followed Egypt, Babylon, Carthage, and others, resounding and great names in Old World history each in its turn drawing to itself the world's wealth and riches, trade and golden treasure, and along with it the world's hate and enmity, envy and covetous rivalry.

Africa yielded its hoards of treasure to the Pharaohs and King Solomon. Then Asia added its quota to the dwellers of Mesopotamia.

Centuries passed slowly, and with them, treasure, wealth, and power rolled westward, and haughty Spain stepped proudly into the picture as the new "Mistress of the World." But not being content with the treasures of the Old World, and having discovered the New World, she proceeded to gather into her treasury its incalculable spoils. Into

Fig. 1. Sketch of the Spanish *Plata Flota* ready to sail from Puerto Plata. Laden with $21,000,000-worth of gold and silver loot from the Spanish colonies along the Caribbean and Gulf Coast, the ships were lost in the terrible hurricane of 1643. Sir William Phipps salvaged nearly $2,000,000 from one of the sunken wrecks in 1687.

Fig. 2. The British frigate *Grosvenor*, carrying a huge treasure cargo of 2,000 silver ingots, 720 gold ingots, and jewels including the fabulous "golden peacocks" from the throne of the Great Mogul, at Delhi, India. It sank August 4, 1782, in Natal Bay, East Africa. In 1952, British salvors recovered nearly $1,000,000-worth of the $5,360,000 treasure and took up residence in Brazil to escape the British government's tax on such recoveries.

Fig. 3. On these forlorn, bleak and treacherous shores of Sable Island, huge waves have shattered more than 750 ships of all types during the past 300 years. On this same island, many pirates, buccaneers, murderers, convicts, beachcombers, renegades and others escaping from society have taken refuge down through the ages. Many of the sunken ships are still resting beneath the waves with an estimated treasure of more than $5,000,000 in gold, silver and other valuables, and millions of dollars in such treasure have been washed up from storms or have been found buried on the shore.

Fig. 4. The famous Lutine Bell, salvaged from *H.M.S. Lutine* which sank off the coast of Holland in 1799. It carried gold specie, valued at $5,500,000, from Yarmouth Roads to Cuxhaven. Many have sought the treasure without success. The bell symbolizes Lloyd's of London to many people because Lloyd's had insured the treasure.

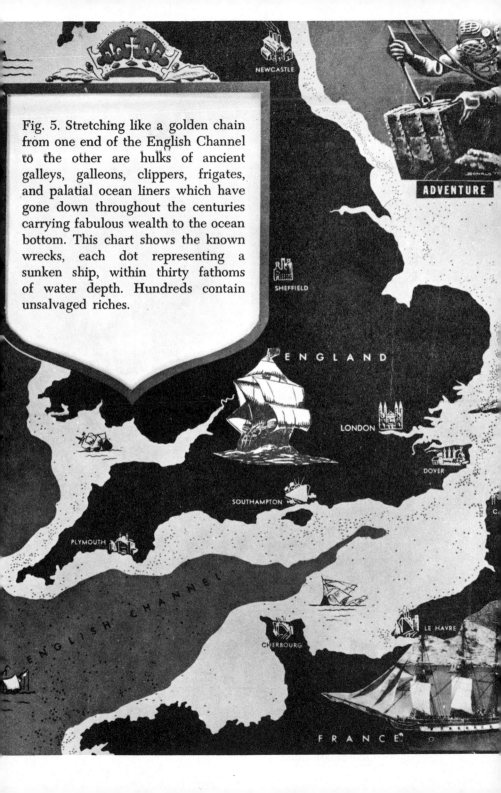

Fig. 5. Stretching like a golden chain from one end of the English Channel to the other are hulks of ancient galleys, galleons, clippers, frigates, and palatial ocean liners which have gone down throughout the centuries carrying fabulous wealth to the ocean bottom. This chart shows the known wrecks, each dot representing a sunken ship, within thirty fathoms of water depth. Hundreds contain unsalvaged riches.

Fig. 6. The sidewheel steamer *Brother Jonathan* was sunk during a terrific storm in 1865, nine miles off Crescent City, California, with $335,000 in gold, silver, and other insured cargo. As yet there has been no salvage operation to recover this treasure. (From early painting.)

Fig. 7. Crude skin diving gear used by native Arab divers in Persian Gulf waters. While searching for wreck sites, the diver gets his air through a tube attached to an animal skin which has been inflated by air—a primitive substitute for air tanks and air hose.

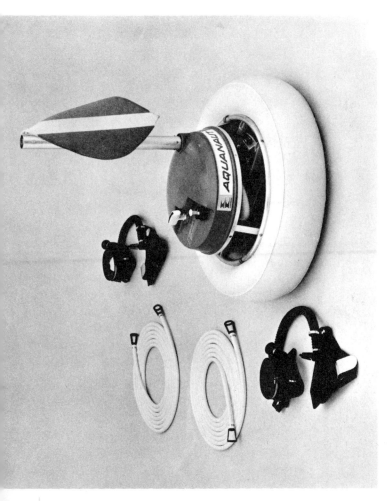

Fig. 8. In contrast to the apparatus shown in Figure 7, the Evinrude Aquanaut is a portable, floating diving unit that feeds air directly to two divers from power-driven compressors mounted in a floating "doughnut." The floating unit follows divers as they swim below, and parallel to the surface of the water, eliminating the need for tanks of air strapped to the back of the diver.

Fig. 9. Reading & Bates' Ocean Engineering Division's Diving Robot used in underwater oil exploration and treasure wreck salvage.

Fig. 10. The latest diving robot devised by the author to penetrate depths beyond the capability of a suited diver.

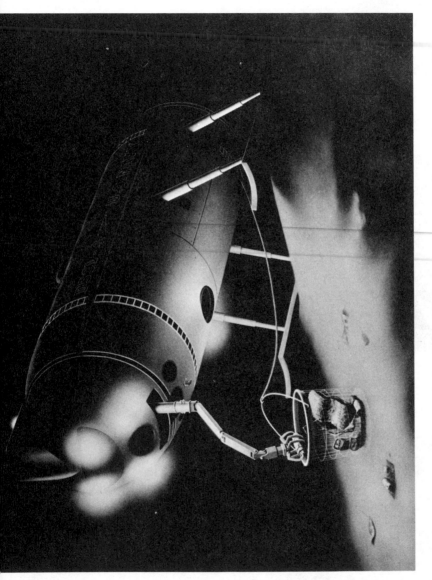

Fig. 11. Artist's concept of the deep submergence search robot under construction by the Lockheed Missiles & Space Company, a division of Lockheed Aircraft Corp., Sunnyvale, California. It is capable of penetrating the ocean depths to 20,000 feet.

the coffers haughty and proud Dons flowed the golden stream from Pizarro's Peruvian treasure-house and Cortés' untold wealth, which, once started, increased astonishingly, and poured forth in ever increasing volume.

Hitherto one pictures the treasure-traffic as being carried on in the Eastern lands by means of caravans over the desert and plain, but not so with the entrance of Spain into the vortex with new sources of riches tapped in her colonial possessions of the New World. It brought a breezy freshness into the age-worn romance, a salt tang of the wide oceans as Spanish naos, galleons, and frigates began to ply the seas laden with golden treasures looted from the Aztecs and the Inca nations.

The cry was *"Westward Ho!"* and from the wondrous New World came fleets of stately galleons and frigates stacked high with chests of gold, silver, and other precious and immense riches. A brave and gallant band they were, Hawkins, Drake, Raleigh, and Oxenham, the brave adventurers who took up the trail which led to Carthagena, Porto Bello, Rio Grande, Nombre de Dias, Hispaniola, and the Spanish Main. They were names that reek with adventure, romance, and treasure-lure! Burning Panama lights the background of the pirates and buccaneers, while the chink of ducats, doubloons, and pieces-of-eight served to drown the ghostly wail of their victims; for gold, silver, and gems galore leaked through the countless wounds, snared the hearts of men and drew them forth to fortune—or to death.

Then time again slowly passed. The arrogant power of Spain dwindled and slackened off, and as the loss of Spain's power disintegrated, there came, in full array, the pirates and the buccaneers—Mansvelt, Morgan, Kidd, Teach— greedy robbers, who like bees drawn to the scent of the golden honey founded hives in ever increasing numbers around the overflowing comb. Their hum and buzz rose louder and louder, until their ceaseless stinging at length paralyzed the harassed workers, and the golden honey soon ceased to flow, the comb sucked empty—decayed. The glory of the Spanish Main vanished with the treasure! Spanish galleons and frigates grew fewer and fewer; the pirates and buccaneers were exterminated, and for a period the lure for treasure gave way to the lust for empire and world power. It became a period for spending rather than for gain, and men and gold were poured into the melting pot and cauldron and melted away. The fate of the world was at stake. India and the Far East became settled; America wrenched herself free from Britain's yoke; Napoleon blazed for a brief moment on the horizon and fell, followed by an era of revival and reconstruction.

The lure of treasure went on! Gold was discovered in California, then Australia, and Canada—then in South Africa, which later turned out to have the richest gold fields in history. Later, from the sweltering plains of Africa's veldt, the cry arose and the call to the ice-bound regions of the mighty Yukon and the great Klondike.

Then came World War I! This was followed by the "depression" of the present century, and once again men began to whisper among themselves the words "treasure" and "gold," and the lure was again flowing through man's veins. The world went off the gold-standard; the precious yellow metal was in demand; the United States government was buying gold. *"Buying gold!"* These words have again caused men to grow restless, and their hearts are anew turning to the lure of the golden magnet today!

Let us descend down into the watery abode of Davy Jones' Locker—into the Old Man of the Sea's treasure-vaults —where still rest those ill-fated galleons, frigates, and other gallant ships which throughout the centuries had carried so much of this once-mined gold and silver treasure, from those early days down through the ages to the present day. Most of those early treasure-bearing craft no longer exist, but their unperishable cargoes of riches remain on the spot where they met their final anchorage, still resting intact with their golden hoards. Let us try to learn something of what became of much of this golden argosy—one-eighth of the world's mined gold and silver treasure—and of the ageless lure which today leads man to brave the undersea depths in his search for such wealth.

Too, let us look through the spectacles of authenticity, our ears listening greedily for the chink of doubloons, ducats, pesos, pieces-of-eight, and other treasure, our eyes ever seeking for these wonderful regions where heroic desperadoes lolled at their ease and captured loot and plunder by the shipload from passing craft sailing the Seven Seas, or for those equally pleasant spots dotting the world's waters wheer more modern treasure-trove still awaits the modern-day underwater salvor and treasure-hunter.

They are still there . . . waiting . . . !

Volumes could be filled with the various tales, more or less fanciful, that have been told about treasure and other precious loot hidden away on remote islands, in sunken ships, and other hiding places in the earth's waters. Fiction writers have not been slow to seize upon such fragments of truth in order to work them into a form of romanticism which will never lose its appeal to the public. However, disregarding fiction of this type, there is no question that quite a number of these treasure-troves were concealed in out-of-the-way spots during the heyday of the pirates and buccaneers. Whether any of these "buried treasure chests" still remain in their earthly hiding places is another question.

But of the existence of ships wrecked in the coastal, lake, and river waters, of which there were many, those which carried fabulous consignments of gold and silver and other valuables, there is no question, although there has been little reported in historical records and marine documents. While there have been untold fortunes recovered by salvage and underwater explorers from hundreds of such treasure-bearing craft, there are still huge numbers that have, so far, defied discovery and recovery. In the waters off almost every continent, concealed within a lake's waters, or a river's muddy bed, or more so, in the depths along coastal waters, useless at present to all and resisting every effort to retrieve them, there still rest riches the worth of which would have to be calculated in hundreds of millions of dollars.

For instance, in most of these waters, lie many a long-submerged treasure-bearing wreck with timbers long years ago rotted, disintegrated, and strewn about amid coral beds, sand spits, and other underwater areas. Here, coins bearing the crowned lion of Holland and the monograms of Spanish, English, French, Dutch royalty, and other insignia still await discovery and retrieval by some fortunate salvor bold enough to go down into the sweep and surge of treacherous depths. Treasure, hidden by pirates and buccaneers, perhaps even by that greatest of all pirates Davy Jones, through accident, storm, hurricane, foundering or other cause; gold ingots, bars of silver, and jewels of fabulous worth waiting for the energetic and adventurous.

Fifty fathoms—three hundred feet—below the surface lies the greater number of these known remaining prizes, but hundreds rest in shallower waters. When most of these vessels sank, the world had no such diving equipment as that which, during the past few years, has come into existence through the achievements of such men as Harry L. Bowdoin,

Simon Lake, and Eugene Romano. Even scuba equipment had not as yet been devised.

But the bottoms of the seas are still unexplored territories, and the treasure-troves of the coninents are again offering a powerful lure of the adventurous! The United States is *"buying both gold and silver today!"* The glory of treasure-hunting has again arrived! And the*"Mighty Underseas Fleets are waiting. . . . !*

Treasure Shipwrecks

UNITED STATES: ATLANTIC COAST

Unidentified Spanish Galleon (1)

FOUNDERED JUNE 12, 1526, off reefs of Cape Fear, North Carolina, carrying down gold and silver bullion and specie amounting to $1,000,000. The vessel was the flagship of Lucas Vasquez de Ayllon.

Tiger (2)

British frigate, flagship of Sir Richard Grenville, foundered June 29, 1585, in twelve fathoms, in Ocracoke Inlet, North Carolina, with an estimated $1,000,000 in gold bullion and specie.

Princess Augusta (3)

British frigate foundered December 27, 1738, off what is known today as the "Hummock," north tip of Sandy Point, Block Island, Rhode Island. The treasure consisted of the possessions and antiques of approximately $100,000 in gold, silver plate and silver specie of the Protestant Palentines, who had been persecuted for their religious beliefs.

Three Spanish Galleons (4)

Three treasure-bearing galleons sank August 18, 1750, in depths ranging from 4 to ten fathoms, of General Juan Manuel de Bonilla's fleet. The flagship *El Salvador* foundered on reefs of Topsail Inlet; the *Nuestra Señora de Guadalupe*, in Ocracoke Inlet! and the *Nuestra Señora de la Soledad*, in Drum Inlet, North Carolina. Estimated total treasure loss exceeded $2,000,000 in gold bullion, silver plate, and specie.

Merlin (5)

British frigate, an eighteen-gun payship for the forces of Admiral Howe, to make payment to the troops at the Battle of Germantown, near Philadelphia, Pa., foundered November 13, 1777, in eighteen fathoms, just offshore of Forts Mercer and Nassau, in the Delaware Channel, New Jersey, with $2,000,000 in gold and silver bullion and specie.

Augusta (6)

British frigate, a sixty-four-gun payship for the forces of Admiral Howe, to make payment to the troops at the Battle of Germantown, near Philadelphia, Pa., foundered November 11, 1777, in sixteen fathoms, just offshore of Forts Mercer and Nassau, in Delaware Channel, New Jersey, with approximately $1,000,000 in gold and silver bullion and specie.

Defense (7)

American frigate payship (privateer) of General Washington's forces in the Battle of the Revolution, sank March 11, 1779, in six fathoms, four miles off Goshen Reef (now Bartlett's Reef), near Waterford, Connecticut, with $200,-000 in gold and silver specie.

Lexington (8)

British frigate payship foundered September 13, 1780, in eleven fathoms, off 138th Street, East River, New York, with $1,800,000 in gold and silver bullion and specie.

Hussar (9)

British frigate payship foundered September 13, 1780, in eight fathoms, between North Brothers Island and 138th Street, East River, New York. The vessel carried down approximately $3,000,000 in gold and silver bullion and specie.

Two Unidentified Spanish Galleons (10)

Foundered in 1784, off Sandbridge, south of Virginia Beach, Virginia, with an estimated $1,000,000 in gold and silver bullion and specie.

Faithful Steward (11)

British frigate foundered July 21, 1785, in fifteen fathoms, two miles northeast of Rehoboth Beach, Delaware, with

$500,000 in gold and silver bullion and specie. Coins still washed ashore.

De Braak (12)

British frigate foundered March 25, 1798, in fourteen fathoms, one mile off lightship at Cape Henlopen, Delaware Bay, Delaware, with $15,000,000 in gold and silver bullion and specie, seventy tons of copper ingots, 80,000 pounds of English gold taken on at Jamaica for the Bank of England, in London, and a consignment of jewels. To date some $200,-000 in coins have been washed ashore off Lewes, Delaware, after storms. Many salvage attempts to locate this vessel's remains have failed.

Five Unidentified Spanish Galleons (13)

Foundered May 25, 1798, in ten fathoms, offshore St. Bernard Inlet, Georgia, with an estimated $1,000,000 in gold and silver bullion and specie.

Juno (14)

Spanish thirty-four-gun frigate foundered in thirty fathoms, on October 29, 1802, on coastal shelf approximately twenty-two miles east of Cape May, New Jersey, with $300,-000 in silver.

Vineyard (15)

American brig foundered December 6, 1830, in six fathoms, two miles southeast of Southampton Light, Long Island, New York, with $54,000 in gold and silver specie consigned to the famous philanthropist and businessman Stephen Girard, of Philadelphia, Pa.

Central America (16)

American steamer foundered September 12, 1857, in fourteen fathoms, four miles off eastern tip of Diamond Shoals, Cape Hatteras, North Carolina, with $2,400,000 in gold bullion, gold ingots and dust consigned to New York banks. The vessel was the first gold ship from the California goldfields to carry Mother Lode bullion to the eastern ports.

Portland (17)

American steamer foundered November 26, 1898, in twenty-seven fathoms, two miles offshore Provincetown, Cape Cod, Massachusetts, carrying down $220,000 in gold and silver specie and $18,000 in jewels and uncut diamonds in bags.

Delaware (18)

American steamer burned to water's edge July 10, 1898, in eleven and a half fathoms, one and a quarter miles off Bayhead, New Jersey, with $250,000 in gold bullion stored in ship's safe.

Harold (19)

American barge. Captain Peter Moore, while lightening his vessel, dumped four hundred tons of metal (silver and lead) ore overboard during storm, September 27, 1903, while en route to the American Smelting & Refining Co. off Sewaren,

Staten Island Sound, New Jersey. Of the 7,678 ingots, 2,938 were recovered. The British and Foreign Insurance Company, Ltd., insured the consignment.

Republic (20)

British steamer foundered January 23, 1909, in thirty-eight fathoms, twenty miles southwest of Nantucket South Shoals Lightship (latitude 40° 25′ 30″ north, longitude 69° 40′ west), with a consignment of gold bullion and silver amounting to approximately $3,000,000. This was the first ship to use radio calls at sea during an emergency.

Mérida (21)

American steamer collided with the *Admiral Farragut*, May 12, 1911, forty-two miles offshore the Virginia Capes, with some $5,500,000 in gold and silver bullion, jewels, and other treasure such as cargo of copper ingots, mahogany logs, etc. Numerous salvage attempts have been made to locate the wreck, but all have failed, notwithstanding many scuba divers' claims.

Arundo (22)

Dutch steamer foundered in 1942, in thirteen fathoms, fifteen miles due east of Shark River Inlet, New Jersey, with $100,000 in gold and silver specie. (Latitude 40° 10′ 25″ north, longitude 73° 40′ 56″ west.)

U-853 (23)

German submarine U-boat, commanded by Captain Helmut Sommer, foundered eight miles off Sandy Point, May 5, 1945, in twenty-one fathoms. The treasure rests off Point Judith, Rhode Island, consisting of some $750,000 in jewels and United States currency, taken from the vaults of the American Traveler's Express Company, in Paris, France, when that city was seized during World War II, and $1,000,000 in mercury.

Andrea Doria (24)

Italian steamer foundered by collision with Swedish motorship *Stockholm*, July 26, 1956, in forty-two and a half fathoms, forty-five miles southeast of Nantucket Island, Mass. Industrial diamonds, fine china, and unknown treasure in three safes.

UNITED STATES: FLORIDA

Santa Margarita (1)

Spanish galleon foundered May 14, 1622, off submerged reef, south side of Upper Matecumbe Key, Florida, with an estimated $3,000,000 in gold and silver bullion and specie.

Nuestra Señora De Atocha (2)

Spanish galleon foundered September 14, 1622, in ten fathoms, off Alligator Reef, Florida, with an estimated $2,-000,000 in gold and silver bullion and specie.

Almirante (3)

Spanish galleon foundered May 14, 1622, in fifteen fathoms, of Alligator Reef, Florida, with an estimated $2,000,-000 in gold and silver bullion and specie.

Almiranta (4)

Spanish galleon foundered June 12, 1656, just off south side of Mimbres Shoals, off Conch Key, Florida, in six fathoms, with an estimated $4,000,000 in Spanish pesos. In 1657, Spanish salvors recovered approximately $1,000,000.

One Unidentified Spanish Galleon (5)

Spanish galleon foundered October 4, 1651, in eight fathoms, off Conch Key, Florida, with an estimated $1,000,-000 in gold and silver bullion and specie.

Two Unidentified Spanish Galleons (6)

Foundered in 1656, off Conch Key, Florida, with an estimated $4,000,000 in gold and silver bullion and specie, in thirteen fathoms. Spanish salvors recovered some $1,000,-000 the following year.

Fourteen Unidentified Spanish Galleons (7)

Foundered June 30, 1715, during hurricane, along the reefs beginning at north end of Carysfort Reefs and extending southward to Vero Beach, Florida, with an estimated $20,000,000 in gold and silver bullion and specie, which had come from Peru, Mexico and other colonial possessions of Spanish America, under Captain-General Don Juan Esteban de Ubilla. To date some $1,500,000 has been salvaged by various salvors.

Capitana (8)

Spanish galleon foundered August 4, 1715, in six fathoms, on Shoals of Palmar de Ayxm, Cape Kennedy, Florida, with an estimated $3,000,000 in gold and silver bullion and specie.

Eleven Unidentified Spanish Galleons (9)

Foundered July 27, 1715, in shallow water between Cape Canaveral and Palm Beach, Florida, with unknown millions in gold and silver bullion and specie. These vessels were a part of the fleet under Captain-General Don Juan Estaban de Ubilla and Captain Don Manuel de Echevez.

El Infanta (10)

Spanish galleon foundered June 28, 1730, in eight fathoms, off Little Conch Reef, Florida, with $1,000,000 in gold and silver and specie. Some salvage recoveries have been made.

Seven Unidentified Spanish Galleons (11)

Foundered June 28, 1730, after crashing against the reefs on south side, between Upper Matecumbe and Long Keys, Florida, in eight fathoms, with an estimated $4,000,000 in gold and silver bullion and specie.

San Fernando (12)

Foundered July 30, 1733, in fourteen fathoms, off south side of Grassy Key, Florida, ten miles northeast of Marathon, with gold and silver bullion and specie estimated at $2,000,000.

San José (13)

Foundered September 30, 1733, in five fathoms, five miles off south side of Grassy Key, Florida, with an estimated $500,000 in gold and silver bullion and specie. Reported found in 1968 by Tom Gurr and Rudolph Palladino.

Almirante (14)

Foundered July 30, 1733, in fifteen fathoms, off Alligator Reef, Florida, with an estimated $1,500,000 in gold and silver bullion and specie.

Aviso Del Consulado (15)

Foundered July 30, 1733, in ten fathoms, off reef at south end Pacific Reefs, Florida, with an estimated $2,000,-000 in gold and silver bullion.

Tres Puentes (16)

Foundered July 21, 1733, in twenty fathoms, off southeast side of Islamorala, between Upper and Lower Matecumbe Keys, about four miles offshore, with an estimated $1,500,000 in gold and silver bullion and specie.

Twenty Unidentified Spanish Galleons (17)

Foundered July 30, 1733, off south side Grassy Key, Florida, in from two to seven fathoms, with gold and silver bullion and specie treasure estimated at $16,000,000. Approximately $12,000,000 has been recovered to date by various salvage operators.

Fly (18)

British frigate sank June 7, 1805, off Little Conch Reef, Key Largo, Florida, with $100,000 in gold and silver specie.

Volador II (19)

Spanish schooner sank May 25, 1815, off Pensacola, Florida, with approximately $100,000 in specie.

Unidentified Pirate Frigate (20)

Foundered December 7, 1819, in four fathoms, on reef in lagoon at mouth of St. George Sound, Franklin county, Florida, with an estimated $200,000 in gold and silver specie filched from some Spanish vessel.

Unidentified American Schooner (21)

Foundered June 12, 1820, just off Cedar Key, Levy county, at south end of Suwannee Sound, Florida, with an estimated $500,000 in gold and silver bullion and specie, in approximately five fathoms. The vessel carried the purchase price for the Territory of Florida, bought from Spain in 1819. Gold coins are constantly being washed ashore.

Gasparilla II (22)

American pirate frigate foundered in twelve fathoms, December 21, 1821, off south end of Gasparilla Island, just off south Boca Grande, in Charlotte Harbor, Florida, with an estimated $1,000,000 in looted gold and silver bullion and specie taken from Spanish vessels. The vessel was owned by José Gaspar, noted renegade and pirate of the period.

Unidentified British Frigate (23)

Foundered December 11, 1829, in twelve fathoms, on reefs four miles off southeast tip of Soldiers Key, Florida, with an estimated $2,000,000 in silver bullion and specie.

Unidentified Schooner (24)

An unidentified schooner carried a consignment of $23,000 in gold, which had been withdrawn from the Charlestown, South Carolina, subtreasury in 1857, to make payment of federal troops sent to Florida to engage the Seminole Indians. The consignment was placed aboard the vessel in large leather pouches by Army paymaster, Major

Jeremiah Y. Dashiell. En route the money was transferred to a smaller craft, which capsized in the outer breakers of the Indian River Inlet. Today the gold has a market value of approximately $198,000.

Korsholm (25)

Swedish steamer foundered in 1942, due south of Cape Canaveral, Florida, with $200,000 in Swedish specie. (Latitude 28° 12′ 10″ north, longitude 80° 29′ 21″ west.) The vessel rests in eight fathoms.

UNITED STATES: GULF AND INLAND

Unidentified Spanish Galleon (1)

Foundered in 1779, in shallow water, off Dernieres Island, in Terrebonne Bay, Louisiana, with $300,000 in gold and silver bullion and specie. Coins, even to this late day, are washed ashore from the remains of the vessel.

Unidentified Spanish Galleon (2)

Spanish galleon foundered in 1781, in four fathoms, off Marsh Island, in Atchafalaga Bay, Louisiana, with an estimated $500,000 in gold and silver bullion and specie.

Unidentified Spanish Galleon (3)

Foundered on east end of Dauphin Island, at extreme entrance of Mobile Bay, Alabama, in shallow water, in 1801,

with gold and silver bullion and specie estimated at nearly
$1,000,000.

San Pedro (4)

Spanish galleon sunk by buccaneer Jean Lafitte, July
5, 1811, in five fathoms, off extreme west end of Padre
Island (formerly known as Isla Blanca), Texas, near Brazos
Santiago Pass, with an estimated $500,000 in gold and silver
bullion and specie.

Santa Rosa (5)

Spanish galleon sunk by buccaneer Jean Lafitte, January
12, 1816, in Matagorda Bay, off Texas. Two million dollars
in silver ingots were conveyed by wagon-train northward to
St. Louis, Missouri. En route Mexican troops gave chase.
When the wagons reached Hendricks Lake, in East Texas,
twenty miles north of Carthage, the six wagons carrying
the bullion were dumped into the lake. In 1920, a group of
Mexicans recovered three silver ingots, the rest still buried
somewhere in the lake's bottom.

Bertrand (6)

American paddlewheel steamer foundered April 1, 1864,
in four fathoms, four miles off Michaelson's Point, near Blair,
Nebraska, with $100,000 in mercury and whiskey. Reported
located in 1969.

S. J. Lee (7)

American sidewheel steamer foundered December 6, 1873, in three fathoms, off Brazos Island bar, Texas, with $100,000 in gold and silver specie.

Paisano (8)

American steamer foundered off St. Joseph Island's, east end of Padre Island chain, in 1873, in four fathoms, with $200,000 in canvas bags, while en route to Galveston, Texas.

Little Fleta (9)

American sidewheel steamer foundered September 5, 1874, in four fathoms, off La Balsa, Texas, with $30,000 in gold and silver specie.

Texas Ranger (10)

American sidewheel steamer foundered June 25, 1875, in three fathoms, during Galveston Flood, on spit off Brazos Island, Texas, with $200,000 in gold and silver specie.

Ida Lewis (11)

American sidewheel steamer foundered June 25, 1875, in four fathoms, during Galveston Flood, off North Breakers' sandbar, Brazos Island, Texas, with $20,000 in gold and silver specie.

Jessie (12)

American sidewheel steamer foundered June 25, 1875, in three fathoms, during Galveston Flood, on sand spit at mouth of Rio Grande River, Texas, with $100,000 in gold and silver specie.

Reine Des Mars (13)

French brig foundered November 15, 1875, in three fathoms, in inside passage off Brazos Island, Texas, with $100,000 in gold and silver specie, liquors and wines from France.

Clara Woodhouse (14)

American sidewheel steamer foundered October 1, 1877, in five fathoms, off North Breakers' sandbar, Brazos Island, Texas, with $80,000 in gold and silver specie.

Maria Theresa (15)

French barque foundered June 15, 1880, in four fathoms, one mile up the Brazos Pass, off west end of Padre Island, Texas, with $210,000 in gold and silver specie, wines and liquors from France.

Carrie A. Thomas (16)

American sidewheel steamer foundered June 16, 1880, in four fathoms, off Rio Grande City, Texas, now buried in the changeable river bed, with \$125,000 in gold and silver specie.

UNITED STATES: WEST COAST

Santo Domingo (1)

Spanish galleon foundered in fall of 1540, in twenty fathoms, five miles off mouth of Escondido Creek, California, with an estimated treasure in gold, silver, and specie of \$3,000,000.

Trinidad (2)

Spanish galleon sank August 12, 1540, in shallow water, off Point La Jolla, between Encinitas and Solano Beach, California, with \$5,000,000 in early Spanish specie, gold bullion, and plundered Aztec gold. A Manila galleon.

San Augustin (3)

Spanish galleon (Manila) foundered in 1594, in eight fathoms, on reefs in Drakes Bay, off Point Reyes, California. The vessel was commanded by Captain Sebastian Cermenon, and carried down an estimated treasure in gold bullion, silver, porcelain, ivory and pearls, valued at \$500,000. Recently numerous coins have been washed ashore.

Unidentified Manila Galleon (4)

Spanish galleon foundered in 1595, in Drakes Bay, off Drakes Beach, Point Reyes, California, at the easterly tip of the peninsula after striking rocks. An estimated treasure in gold and silver bullion and specie valued at approximately $1,000,000 sank. In 1941, some relics and artifacts supposedly a part of the galleon were recovered by University of California anthropologists.

San Pedro (5)

Manila galleon foundered June 4, 1598, in fourteen fathoms, on reef off Arrow Point, Santa Catalina Island, California, with $2,000,000 in gold and silver bullion and specie.

Nuestra Señora De Ayuda (6)

Manila galleon of 230 tons struck rock reef on west side of Catalina Island, California, June 3, 1641, carrying down gold and silver bullion and specie amounting to $500,000.

Unidentified Manila Galleon (7)

Foundered on reefs at outer point of Cortez Bank, now called Bishop Rock, California, July 2, 1717, in three fathoms, with $200,000 in gold and silver bullion and specie.

Santa Rosa (8)

Manila galleon sank October 3, 1717, in twenty fathoms, on reef off Bishop Rock, south southeast Cortez Bank, California, with an estimated $700,000 in gold and silver bullion and specie.

Unidentified Manila Galleon (9)

Foundered in shallow water three miles off Clatsop Beach, Oregon, August 4, 1725, with $100,000 (estimated) in gold and silver specie and plate.

Sebastián (10)

Manila galleon foundered January 7, 1754, in thirty-six fathoms, two miles off northeast end of Santa Catalina Island, California, with gold and silver bullion estimated at $1,500,000. To date $1,000,000 has been recovered by salvage group.

Unidentified Manila Galleon (11)

Manila galleon crashed on Nehalem Spit, near Neah-Kah-Nie Mountain, July 7, 1760, with unknown treasure cargo.

Unidentified Manila Galleon (12)

Foundered October 11, 1801, in twelve fathoms, off northwest tip of San Miguel Island, thirty-seven miles due west of Santa Barbara, California, with an unknown treasure in gold, silver, and specie.

Santa Marta (13)

Manila galleon foundered August 12, 1852, in shallow water, off west side of Catalina Island, California, with gold and silver bullion valued at $500,000.

Santa Cecilia (14)

Manila galleon sank September 14, 1852, in twelve fathoms, three miles north northwest off Ship's Rock, California, with $200,000 in gold and silver specie.

Yankee Blade (15)

American steamer foundered October 1, 1854, in fourteen fathoms, off Honda's Bridge Rock, north side of Point Arguello Reef, California. The wreck rests one and a half miles from shore, and was commanded by Captain Harry Randell. The vessel carried $153,000 in gold bullion from the Mother Lode goldfields, plus specie shipped by Page, Bacon & Co., in heavy steel vault. Some reports claim this vessel carried $1,500,000.

Donna Maria (16)

Swedish brig foundered May 23, 1854, in shallow water, forty miles south of Cape Mendocino, California, with cargo of lumber and $40,000 in specie.

Brother Jonathan (17)

American sidewheel steamer foundered July 30, 1865, off Seal Rocks, St. George Reefs, California, eight miles west of Crescent City, California. The vessel carried down $335,-000 in gold and silver bullion, specie and whiskey.

Pacific (18)

American sidewheel steamer sank in collision with steamer *Orpheus*, November 4, 1875, off Cape Flattery, Washington, with $79,220 in gold and silver specie in master's strongbox.

San José (19)

Manila galleon sank June 31, 1875, in four fathoms, at mouth of the Nehalem River, Oregon, approximately two hundred yards from open sea, with $100,000 in gold and silver specie.

Mollie Stevens (20)

American steamboat foundered June 10, 1878, in two fathoms, in Owens Lake (now dried up), California. The lake is eleven miles northwest of Lone Pine. The cargo was gold and silver ore, valued at approximately $200,000. The vessel was a small steamboat used for ore-carrying from mines. It capsized and sank in the lake, in Inyo county, with four members of the crew dying of thirst in the desert. Today the lake is a dry bed bordering on Highway #395, west of Death Valley, and ten miles northwest of Lone Pine. Several years ago the rusted propeller, decayed lifeboat, anchor, and some gold ore samples were unearthed from under the soft soda crust.

Bremen (21)

American steamer sank off south shore of Farallon Islands, off the entrance to the Golden Gate, in 1883. The cargo consisted of Scotch whiskey and $60,000 in specie, which rests on rocky ledge in deep water.

Besse (22)

American bark foundered July 23, 1886, in ten fathoms, on Peacock Spit, off Besse Buoy, near Cape Hancock, Oregon. Cargo of steel rails and $75,000 in specie.

Respigadera (23)

British steamer struck rocks off Point Fermin, California, in 1888, with $40,000 in specie.

Kathleen (24)

American steamer sank in 1901, off Douglass Island, Alaska, carrying down in deep water $2,000,000 in gold.

San Rafael (25)

American steamer sank November 30, 1901, in twenty fathoms off west side Alcatraz Island, California, with $40,000 in specie.

Condor (26)

British sloop-of-war, of 980-tons, sank in December 1901, in forty-two fathoms, off Tatoosh Island, forty miles northwest of Cape Flattery, Washington, with $100,000 in specie and some gold bullion. In May, 1949, fishermen hauled up in their net the vessel's two-hundred-pound binnacle.

City of Rio De Janeiro (27)

American steamer foundered February 22, 1901, in sixty-two fathoms, off Point Fort, on One Mile Rock, Land's End, California. A gold consignment in specie of $75,000, Chinese silver of $2,000,000, and $37,000 in jewelry is reported to have gone down with the steamer. However, it has been said by an expert diver that "most of the gold and silver reputed to be aboard was loaded on her twenty years after she sank." In 1937, Bill Wood, a local diver brought up a lifeboat plate supposedly that of the vessel; in 1956, A. A. Mikalow, of Oakland, California, located the wreck site, and recently obtained an exclusive claim for early operations.

Islander (28)

British steamer foundered August 15, 1901, in thirty-eight fathoms, in Taku Inlet, Icy Point, Stephens Passage, Alaska, with $3,000,000 in gold bullion, nuggets, and gold-dust. The vessel broke up in two parts. The gold was a consignment from the Alaska and Klondike Territory gold-fields. Salvaged to date, $240,000. Beached in Green's Cove, Admiralty Island.

H. J. Cochrane (29)

American steamer foundered in 1911, in twelve fathoms, on southwest point of Angel Island, San Francisco Bay, California, with $96,000 in gold bullion. The wreck site was reported located by A. A. Mikalow, Oakland, California.

Cuba (30)

American steamer foundered September 9, 1923, in ten fathoms, off southwest end San Miguel Island, thirty-seven miles due west of Santa Barbara, California, with gold and silver bullion valued at $400,000.

San Juan (31)

American steamer sank off Pigeon Point, fifty miles south of San Francisco, California, August 29, 1929, with gold and silver bullion and specie valued at $200,000.

Vazlav Vorovsky (32)

Russian steamer pounded to pieces April 3, 1941, on Peacock Spit, just below Cape Disappointment, Washington, with gold, silver and specie, and heavy machinery for Vladivostok, Russia, valued at $1,750,000, in fifteen fathoms.

Henry Bergh (33)

American steamer foundered May 31, 1944, in thirty-six fathoms, off northwest side of the Farallone Islands, California, with $40,000 in specie and military consignment.

Drexel Victory (34)

American steamer foundered January 19, 1947, off Peacock Spit, below Cape Disappointment, one-quarter mile due west of Buoy #6, Washington, with gold and silver specie valued at $60,000.

Fernstream (35)

British motorship foundered December 25, 1952, in twenty-two fathoms, while in collision with steamer *Hawaiian Rancher*, off southwest side Alcatraz Island, San Francisco Bay, California. The vessel carried down $22,000 in specie, and a cargo valued at $6,000,000.

Diamond Knot (36)

American motorship sank August 11, 1947 in twenty-two fathoms, off Race Rocks, Crescent Bay, Washington, with cargo of $30,000 in specie and a treasure in tinned salmon and fish oil in drums, half of which has been recovered to date.

Jacob Luckenbach (37)

American steamer foundered July 4, 1953, in thirty-five fathoms, seven miles southwest off San Francisco Lightship anchorage, California, with $52,000 in specie and steel cargo.

Miscellaneous Wrecks (38)

More than six hundred ships were lost at the mouth of the Columbia River, among which were eighty-odd treasure-bearing vessels, whose gold and silver consignments are estimated to exceed $100,000,000. Among these are known to be numerous Manila galleons and coastal craft carrying gold, silver, ivory, jewels, etc., and many were laden with gold bullion from the California Mother Lode country goldfields.

Between Tillamook Head and Clatsop, Oregon, once known as the "Graveyard of Ships," more than one hundred and fifty wrecked-ship remains rest beneath the waters just offshore, many of which carried consignments of gold bullion and ingots from the California goldfields.

Off Point Arguello, California, the remains of numerous treasure-bearing still rest which, due to the difficulties of recovery, still contain their cargoes of gold and silver and other valuables.

UNITED STATES: THE GREAT LAKES

Griffin (1)

French shallop, of forty tons, foundered in September, 1679, on the reefs off Birch Island, five miles west of Thessalon, Ontario, Canada, in eight fathoms, with $12,000 in gold specie. The shallop was the craft of the French explorer Robert Cavalier de la Salle. Today the remains, if found, would be a museum relic of great historical worth.

Jean Florin (2)

French frigate foundered July 2, 1721, in twelve fathoms, ten to fifteen miles northeast off Erie, Pennsylvania, in Lake Erie, with $500,000 in gold and silver bullion and specie.

Le Blanc Henri (3)

French frigate foundered June 17, 1764, off rocks of Wolfe Island spit, near Kingston, Canada, in Lake Ontario, with $100,000 in gold and silver bullion and specie.

Ontario (4)

British sloop-of-war payship foundered November 23, 1783, in twelve fathoms, four and a half miles northeast of Oswego, New York, in Lake Ontario, with a consignment of $500,000 in gold and silver bullion and specie.

Erie (5)

American steamer foundered August 9, 1841, in nine and a half fathoms, 4 miles off Silver Creek, near Brandt Erie county, not far from Buffalo, New York, in Lake Erie, with $100,000 in specie and seventy-five barrels of whiskey. Some recovery was made by a Buffalo salvage firm.

Kent (6)

American steamer foundered August 12, 1845, in sixteen fathoms, seven and a half miles southeast of Point Pelee, in Lake Erie, with $65,000 in gold and silver specie.

Lexington (7)

American steamer foundered November 19, 1846, in twelve fathoms, four miles off Point Moullie, in Detroit River, Lake Erie, with $100,000 in gold specie and 125 barrels of whiskey.

Chesapeake (8)

American steamer foundered June 9, 1846, in seven fathoms, three miles due north off Conneaut, Ohio, in Lake Erie, with $8,000 in gold and silver specie.

Anthony Wayne (9)

American steamer foundered April 18, 1850, in eleven fathoms, six and a half miles northwest of Vermillion, New York, in Lake Erie, with $96,000 in specie and wine and 330 barrels of whiskey.

Atlantic (10)

American sidewheel steamer foundered August 20, 1852, in twenty-seven fathoms, due to collision three and a half miles east of Long Point, Ontario tip, in Lake Erie, with $60,000 gold and silver specie and barrels of whiskey.

Superior (11)

American steamer foundered October 29, 1856, in nine fathoms, two and a half miles off Grand Island, Michigan, in Lake Superior, with $40,000 in gold and silver specie, and 216 barrels of whiskey.

Northerner (12)

American steamer foundered April 18, 1856, five miles off Gratiot Light, in Lake Huron, with $25,000 in gold and silver specie and sixty barrels of whiskey.

Sunbeam (13)

American steamer foundered September 28, 1863, in twenty-two fathoms, three miles east of Copper Harbor, off Keweenaw Point, in Lake Superior, with $10,000 in specie and 112 barrels of whiskey.

Manistee (14)

American steamer foundered November 16, 1863, in eighteen fathoms, three miles east offshore of Eagle River, Michigan, in Lake Superior, with $35,000 in specie, eighty tons of copper ingots, and twenty tons of railroad iron.

Westmoreland (15)

American steamer foundered December 7, 1854, in fourteen fathoms, two miles off Sleeping Bear Point, Michigan, in Lake Michigan, with $95,000 in specie, steel, and copper ingots.

Pewabic (16)

American steamer foundered August 9, 1865, in twenty fathoms, two miles off Thunder Bay Island, near Alpena, Michigan, in Lake Huron, with $250,000 in gold and silver specie, and three hundred tons of copper ingots.

R. G. Coburn (17)

American steamer foundered October 15, 1871, in twenty fathoms, three miles off the north entrance to Saginaw Bay, Lake Huron, with $105,000 in gold specie and copper ore ingots valued at $75,000.

City of Detroit (18)

American steamer foundered December 4, 1863, in sixteen fathoms, two miles offshore north of Barcelona, New York, in Lake Erie, with $100,000 in gold and silver specie, and a like amount in copper ingots.

Young Sion (19)

American steamer foundered June 13, 1881, in six fathoms, two miles off the mouth of Walnut Creek, in Lake Erie, with $225,000 in gold and silver specie, and consignment of railroad iron.

Unidentified Legendary Mystery Ship (20)

A legendary mystery ship foundered in 1884, off Poverty Island, near Escanaba, Michigan, with $4,500,000 in gold bullion and specie.

Algoma (21)

Canadian steamer foundered November 7, 1885, in twenty-one fathoms, one-half mile off south shore Royale Island, four miles north of Rock Harbor, in Lake Superior, with $16,000 in specie, steel, and copper ingots.

Seabird (22)

American steamer foundered April 9, 1868, in nine fathoms, seven and a half miles east of Waukegan, Michigan, in Lake Michigan, with $40,000 in gold and silver specie, banknotes and sixty-six barrels of whiskey.

Vernon (23)

American steamer foundered October 29, 1887, in fourteen fathoms, three miles off Two Rivers, Wisconsin, in Lake Michigan, with $30,000 in gold and silver specie.

Glendora (24)

Canadian schooner foundered November 19, 1887, two and a half miles southwest of Amherst Island, Ontario, Canada, in Lake Ontario, with $60,000 in gold and silver specie.

Bruno (25)

American steamer foundered November 13, 1890, in ten fathoms, one and a half miles off Smith Point, Cockburn Island, in Lake Huron, with $35,000 in gold and silver specie and 130 barrels of whiskey.

Dean Richmond (26)

American steamer foundered October 14, 1893, in twenty fathoms, four miles east of Van Buren Point, off the south shore, New York, in Lake Erie, with $141,000 in gold and silver bullion, specie, and 220 tons of pig zinc.

Chicora (27)

American steamer foundered January 2, 1895, in ten fathoms, nine miles southwest of St. Joseph, Michigan, in Lake Michigan, with $50,000 in gold and silver specie and 120 barrels of whiskey.

Joseph S. Fay (28)

American steamer foundered October 19, 1902, in twelve fathoms, six miles off Sand Island, in Saginaw Bay, Lake Huron, with $16,500 in gold and silver specie, steel and copper ingots.

Marquette & Bessemer No. 2 (29)

American car-ferry foundered December 7, 1909, in twelve fathoms, nine miles east of Conneaut, Ohio, in Lake

Erie, with a loss of $65,000 in gold and silver specie, and iron railroad cars.

Clarion (30)

American steamer foundered December 8, 1909, in eleven fathoms, seven miles southeast of Point Moullie, near mouth of the Detroit River, in Lake Erie, with $120,000 in gold and silver bullion and specie, and twelve locomotives valued at $300,000.

Cleveco (31)

American barge foundered December 2, 1943, in five fathoms, three and a half miles east of Cleveland, off Euclid Beach shore, Ohio, in Lake Erie, with $80,000 in gold and silver specie, and 1,000,000 gallons of fuel oil in steel drums.

CANADA

Griffin (1)

French shallop foundered September 12, 1679, in eight fathoms, on Birch Island Reefs, five miles west of Thessalon, Ontario, at eastern entrance to St. Joseph Channel, in Lake Huron, with $12,000 in gold specie. This relic was the forty-ton shallop of the French explorer Robert Cavalier de la Salle, and its recovery would be for historical purposes only.

Feversham (2)

British frigate foundered October 7, 1711, off Scatari Island, twelve miles east of Louisburg, Cape Breton, in fourteen fathoms. One of a fleet under command of Captain Sir Hovenden Walker, with $500,000 in gold, silver and specie, and Dutch silver daalders. Located in 1968 by scuba-diving group of Alex Storm, Adrian Richard, and Harvey MacLeod, with some recoveries.

La Libertie (3)

French frigate foundered December 11, 1719, in twelve fathoms, two miles off St. Esprit, Nova Scotia, Canada, with $500,000 in gold and silver bullion and specie.

Le Chameau (4)

French naval transport payship foundered August 26, 1725, in twelve fathoms, off rocks between Portenove Island and Louisburg, Nova Scotia, Canada, with $4,000,000 in French gold and silver bullion and specie. In 1965, a group of Canadian scuba divers—Alex Storm, Dave MacEachern, and Harvey MacLeod—recovered approximately $700,000 in gold and silver coins, which the Canadian courts are holding pending a decision.

Essex (5)

British frigate foundered March 12, 1741, in twelve fathoms, in channel off east side Deadmen's Island, Magalena Islands, Cape Breton Island, with $200,000 in gold and silver specie.

Tilbury (6)

British frigate foundered June 11, 1751, in eleven fathoms, a few miles offshore between Baleine and Scatari Islands, Cape Breton, Nova Scotia, Canada. The vessel was the payship of Admiral Edward Boscanen's squadron, and carried $500,000 in gold and silver specie. In 1939, fishermen dragged up a few gold sovereigns from the narrow strait between the islands.

Le Blanc Henri (7)

French frigate foundered June 17, 1764, off rocks of Wolfe Island spit, southwest Amherst Island, Ontario, Lake Ontario, Canada, with $100,000 in gold and silver specie.

Barbadoes (8)

British frigate foundered in 1812, in seven fathoms, on sand spit off East Light, Sable Island, Nova Scotia, with $500,000 in gold and silver bullion and specie.

L'Americaine (9)

French frigate foundered December 6, 1822, in nine fathoms, on sand spit off south end Wallace Lake, Sable Island, Nova Scotia, Canada, with $1,000,000 in gold and silver bullion and specie.

Marshall Wellington (10)

British bark foundered in 1823, off north tip sandbar of Sable Island, Nova Scotia, Canada, with $200,000 in gold and silver specie.

Fulwood (11)

British schooner foundered in 1828, off the Isthmus of Langlade, between St. Pierre and Miquelon Islands, with $300,000 in gold bullion and specie. It is reported that the crew mutinied afterward and carried the chests of treasure ashore where they buried them on the isthmus.

Eagle (12)

American ship foundered in 1835 off outer sand spit of Sable Island, Nova Scotia, Canada, with $100,000 in gold and silver specie.

Glenaora (13)

Canadian schooner foundered November 19, 1887, in shallow water, three and a half miles southwest of Amherst Island, Ontario, Lake Ontario, with $60,000 in gold and silver specie.

Bruno (14)

American steamer foundered November 13, 1890, in ten fathoms, one and a half miles off Smith Point, Cockburn Island, Lake Huron, with $35,000 in specie and 130 barrels of whiskey.

Eric (15)

American steamer foundered in 1912, off outer sand spit, in Wallace Lake, Sable Island, Nova Scotia, Canada, with $300,000 in gold and silver bullion and specie.

Independence Hall (16)

American steamer foundered in 1942, in ten fathoms, on sand spit off north tip of Sable Island, Nova Scotia, Canada, with $100,000 in gold and silver specie.

Miscellaneous (17)

The records show that more than seven hundred frigates, barks, brigs, steamers, and other vessels have been sunk on Sable Island's reefs and sand spits during the past three hundred years; there are wrecks of all description, including numerous treasure-bearing craft. The island is known to seafaring men as the "Graveyard of the North Atlantic." Many millions of dollars have been recovered from some of these wrecks.

Off the French islands of Pierre and Miquelon, and at the mouth of the St. Lawrence River, twelve miles from Newfoundland, especially along the Isthmus of Langlade, more than six hundred sunken shipwrecks dot the outer harbor waters.

MEXICO AND LATIN AMERICA

Unidentified Spanish Nao (1)

Foundered in 1555, five miles north of Veracruz, Mexico, with 300,000 pesos in silver.

Larga (2)

Foundered June 7, 1628, in seven fathoms, northeast of San Juan de Ulua, near Veracruz, Mexico, with $400,000 pesos in silver. Approximately $100,000 is remaining of the Spanish frigate, after an early salvage operation.

Almiranta (3)

Manila galleon foundered June 3, 1631, in twenty-one fathoms, off Garadine, in Gulf of San Miguel, Panama, with $2,000,000 in gold bullion, silver, and specie from Callao, Peru.

Draecke (4)

Dutch frigate foundered June 12, 1689, in ten fathoms, one mile off south tip Tiburon Island, Sonora, Mexico, in Gulf of California, with $1,000,000 in gold and silver bullion, specie, and pearls. Even at this late day, after heavy storms, Dutch coins are found along the shores of the island.

Unidentified Spanish Galleon (5)

Foundered June 26, 1765, twelve miles south southeast of Campeche, Bay of Campeche, Yucatan, Mexico, with $2,300,000 in gold and silver bullion.

Santa Marta (6)

Spanish frigate of thirty-eight guns foundered June 11, 1780, in shallow water, in Campeche Bay, Mexico, with $200,000 in gold and silver bullion and specie.

Dragon II (7)

Spanish frigate of sixty guns, foundered on rocks of Najo Nuevo, between Havana and Veracruz, on reef, May 2, 1783, with $200,000 in six chests.

Water Witch (8)

British frigate foundered June 12, 1793, just offshore south tip of Ambergris Island, British Honduras, with $1,700,000 in gold and silver bullion and specie.

Leviathan (9)

British frigate foundered March 11, 1799, in twenty-five fathoms, two miles west of Puerto Cortes, Honduras, with $200,000 in gold and silver bullion and gems.

Ifigonia (10)

Spanish frigate of thirty-eight guns, foundered June 12, 1818, on submerged rocks at mouth of Yucatan Channel, Mexico, with approximately $30,000 in specie. The vessel was under the command of Captain Alejo Gutierrez de Rubalcava when she struck on the Iphigenia rocks.

Juan Baptista (11)

Spanish galleon foundered July 21, 1822, in shallow water, on shoals one mile off Lighthouse Reef, Turneffe Island, British Honduras, with $800,000 in gold and silver bullion and specie.

Golden Gate (12)

American steamer foundered July 27, 1862, in six fathoms, one-half mile offshore, fourteen miles north of Manzanillo, Colima Province, Mexico, with $1,577,760 in gold bullion and specie. In 1900, Duncan Johnston, of Providence, R. I., recovered $10,000; later some $1,030,000 was salvaged by various divers.

Golden City (13)

American steamer foundered February 22, 1870, in nine fathoms, off Cape San Lazaro, Santa Margarita Island, Baja California, Mexico, with $500,000 in gold and silver bullion and specie.

Sacramento (14)

American steamer foundered December 5, 1872, in nine fathoms, on Sacramento Reef, not far off San Geronimo Island, Baja California, Mexico, with $2,000,000 in gold and silver bullion and specie. $390,000 has been salvaged.

Lea (15)

American sidewheel steamer foundered June 10, 1880, in three fathoms, one-half mile off river mouth at Matamoras, Mexico, with consignment of $100,000 in gold and silver specie.

Enterprise (16)

British schooner foundered March 4, 1892, in eleven fathoms, against rock cliffs one-half mile off Villamil, south side of Galapagos Island, with $750,000 in gold and silver bullion and specie.

Emily P. Wright (17)

American steamer foundered in 1914, in six fathoms, on reefs at entrance to Laguna Madre, off Point San Rafael, Mexico, with $40,000 in gold and silver specie.

Colombia (18)

American steamer foundered September 13, 1931, off Point Tasco, Baja California, Mexico, after leaving Mazatlan with $320,000 in gold and silver bullion and specie. The vessel first stranded, then foundered; her passengers were picked up from life boats by steamers *San Mateo* and *La Perla*. Salvaged to date, $200,000.

CARIBBEAN AND WEST INDIES *

Golden Hinde (1)

Spanish galleon foundered July 14, 1502, in approximately twenty fathoms, some four miles northeast of Cape Haitien (what is known today as Haiti), on treacherous reefs, carrying down an estimated $5,000,000 in gold and silver bullion and specie.

El Dorado (2)

Spanish galleon foundered in 1502, in twenty fathoms, between Mayaguez and Mona Islands, Puerto Rico, with $3,000,000 in gold and silver bullion and specie.

Twenty-Six Spanish Galleons (3)

A Spanish plate fleet consisting of galleons, naos, and patches foundered in twenty-four fathoms, July 4, 1502, between Mayaguez and Mona Islands, Puerto Rico, with an estimated $7,000,000 in gold and silver bullion and specie.

---

* No. 36 describes the submerged city of Jamestown.

Santa Clara (4)

Spanish galleon foundered June 18, 1597, in twenty-two fathoms, twenty miles east of shoals off Cape Haitien, Haiti, with an estimated $15,000,000 in gold and silver bullion and specie.

Unidentified Spanish Galleon (5)

Sunk 1584, in four fathoms, on outer edge of Bermuda's barrier reefs, with $1,000,000 in gold, silver and specie. Was located by Harry Cox, of Bermuda, and recovered some pieces-of-eight, fifteen-foot gold chain, gold rings, an astrolabe, and other jewelry.

San Fernando (6)

Spanish galleon foundered February 13, 1597, in thirty fathoms, two miles off Point du Cap, at extreme northern tip of Santa Lucia Island, Santa Lucia Channel, Leeward Islands, with $20,000,000 in gold and silver bullion and specie.

Unidentified Spanish Galleon (7)

Foundered September 8, 1628, in twelve fathoms, two miles off outer harbor of Matanzas, Matanzas Bay, Cuba, with an estimated $1,000,000 in gold and silver bullion and specie.

Eleven Unidentified Spanish Galleons (8)

A fleet of eleven galleons was sunk September 8, 1628, by the Dutch pirate Piet Heyn, in twelve fathoms, just off shore Matanzas harbor, Matanzas Bay, Cuba, with $30,000,-000 in gold and silver bullion and specie.

Spanish Plate Fleet (9)

Commanded by Admiral Juan de Villavicencio, fourteen Spanish galleons foundered November 16, 1643, in hurricane, in approximately sixty to 120 fathoms, in the Silver Bank region, at the extreme southeastern tip of the Bahamas. The fleet carried down approximately $21,000,000 in gold and silver bullion and specie. In 1687, Captain (later Sir) William Phipps recovered $1,500,000 from one of the wrecks, for which service he was later knighted by the king of England, and appointed royal governor of the Massachusetts Colony.

Unidentified Spanish Galleon (10)

Foundered November 4, 1670, on reefs off southern tip of the Ambrogian Reefs, in the Silver Bank Passage, at the extreme end of the Bahamas, with an estimated $7,000,000 in gold and silver bullion and specie.

Santa Paula (11)

Spanish galleon foundered August 12, 1679, in twelve fathoms, three miles southeast of Point Guanal Island, Isle of Pines, Cuba, with $3,500,000 in gold and silver bullion and specie. Sixty thousand dollars was recovered in 1936.

San Sebastián (12)

Spanish galleon foundered December 9, 1683, in eight fathoms, off southwest side of Rackhams Cay, approximately fifteen miles south of Port Royal, Jamaica, with $1,500,000 in gold and silver bullion, specie and plate.

San Rafael (13)

Spanish galleon foundered June 11, 1691, in fourteen fathoms, one and a half miles off eastern end of Guanal Island, Isle of Pines, Cuba, with $3,000,000 in gold and silver bullion and specie.

Santo Domingo (14)

Spanish galleon foundered April 21, 1715, two miles off Cay Largo, Canarreos Archipelago, Isle of Pines, Cuba, with $7,000,000 in gold and silver bullion and specie.

El Capitan (15)

Spanish galleon foundered December 4, 1717, in three fathoms, one and a half miles southeast Southern Cay, off Gorda Cay, Bahamas, with an estimated $2,000,000 in gold bullion, silver plate, and specie. In 1936, $81,500 was recovered.

San Pedro (16)

Spanish galleon foundered July 22, 1719, in four fathoms, off Gorda Cay, near Sandy Point, Abaca Island, Bahamas, with an estimated $500,000 in gold and silver bullion and specie. In 1936, $20,000 was recovered.

Santa Elena (17)

Spanish galleon foundered November 12, 1719, one and a half miles off Bonefish Hole, East Bimini, Bimini Island, with an estimated $1,200,000 in gold and silver bullion and specie.

Genovése (18)

Spanish frigate foundered August 23, 1730, in approximately three fathoms, off Pedro Cays, near Banner Reef, Pedro Bank, a two-mile-long, two-hundred-feet-wide cay. This vessel was the flagship of Captain Francisco Guiral, and carried down $3,500,000 in gold and silver bullion and specie. In 1901, 186 gold coins and three bars of silver, each weighing in excess of twenty-six pounds were recovered and sold for $100,000; in 1960, and later years, approximately $1,800,000 was recovered by various salvage groups.

Capitana (19)

Spanish frigate foundered October 4, 1731, on reefs off Terre de Haut, Guadeloupe, in Leeward Islands, with approximately $1,000,000 in gold and silver bullion, and some specie.

Unidentified Spanish Galleon (20)

Struck rocks and foundered August 11, 1731, three miles northeast of Nueva Gerona Island, in Gulf of Batabama, Isle of Pines, Cuba, in sixteen fathoms, with an estimated $1,000,000 in gold and silver bullion and specie.

San Ignacio (21)

Spanish nao foundered August 11, 1742, in shallow water, on southeast side of the Anegada reefs, Virgin Islands, with $500,000 in gold bullion, specie, and crude diamonds.

San Ignacio (22)

Spanish galleon foundered August 22, 1733, in eight fathoms, twelve miles offshore Northeast Cay, Pedro Cays, Jamaica, carrying down $300,000 in gold and silver specie and silver plate.

Eleven Unidentified Spanish Galleons (23)

Foundered in 1734, in twenty fathoms, off Beef Island, at extreme eastern end of Tortala, British Virgin Islands, with an estimated $4,000,000 in gold and silver bullion and specie.

La Trinidad (24)

Spanish galleon foundered July 7, 1738, in twenty-two fathoms, on rocks off Beef Island, at extreme eastern end of

Tortala, British Virgin Islands, with $1,000,000 in gold and silver bullion and specie.

La Victoria (25)

Spanish frigate foundered in 1738, just offshore of the northeastern end of Anegada Island, British Virgin Islands, with an estimated $1,750,000 in gold and silver bullion and specie. The vessel was a large Spanish warship.

San José (26)

Spanish galleon sank December 1738, in five fathoms, off Dead Man's Chest Islet, British Virgin Islands, with approximately $2,500,000 in gold and silver bullion and specie.

Soledad (27)

Spanish galleon foundered November 14, 1739, in six fathoms, on offshore reefs one-half mile off Anegada Island, British Virgin Islands, with an estimated $3,000,000 in gold and silver bullion and specie.

El Salvador (28)

Spansh galleon foundered December 3, 1744, in nine fathoms, on rocks off Dead Man's Chest, British Virgin Islands, with an estimated $700,000 in gold and silver bullion and specie.

Invencible (29)

Spanish frigate 1,300 tons, foundered in Havana harbor, June 30, 1741, heavily laden with gold and silver bullion and specie amounting to about $1,000,000. To date only some $20,000 has been recovered, and this by accident.

Unidentified French Frigate (30)

Foundered April 12, 1782, in eight fathoms, one mile off outer harbor of Roseau, Dominica Island, in Leeward Islands, with $380,000 (estimated) in gold and silver bullion and French specie. In 1936, $69,000 was recovered.

Infanta (31)

An eighteen-gun barkentine under the command of Spanish Captain Casimiro de la Madrid struck reefs off Inagua Chica, Bahamas, August 12, 1788, and foundered in seventeen fathoms, carrying down approximately $200,000 in gold and silver bullion and specie.

Palas (32)

Spanish frigate foundered in 1797, in three fathoms, on reefs called Colorados de la Cruz del Padre, just north of Cruz del Padre, with $300,000 in gold and silver specie.

Don Carlos (33)

Spanish galleon foundered November 21, 1812, in nine fathoms, four and a half miles offshore of outer harbor of Matanzas, Matanzas Bay, Cuba, with $1,000,000 in gold doubloons, pieces-of-eight, silver plate, and specie.

Almirante (34)

Spanish bark, under command of Admiral Ignacio Chacón, foundered in 1821, near Cayo de Santo Domingo, in twenty fathoms, with $300,000 in gold and silver bullion and specie.

Virgin Island Wrecks (35)

More than 180 wrecks rest in the coral barrier sea bottom just south of Anegada Passage, from Saba Bank southward to St. Vincent Passage. Mostly trading craft from Europe, and slavers from Africa, they sunk during the eighteenth and nineteenth centuries while searching for the narrow passages of the Mona Channel leading to the larger islands. Many of them, in addition to carrying cargoes of slaves, carried huge gold and silver consignments.

Among the richest areas in the Caribbean and West Indies are those off the southwest coast of Cuba, Isle of Pines; off Cape Antonio at the western end of Cuba; off the islands and reefs of both the Windward and Leeward Passages; among the reefs off Bermuda, the Cayman Islands, and the outer waters of the larger ports of the West Indies, such as Puerto Plata, Kingston Harbor, and channels leading out from Nassau.

Sunken City (36)

In 1680, the city of Jamestown, five miles from the present Charlestown, on Nevis Island, in the Leeward Islands, was swept into the outer offshore waters by earthquakes and deluge, taking down the relics of the palace and churches together with gold and silver stored in the warehouses waiting shipment to the Continent. From time to time, divers have come upon these treasures, and brought to the surface gold ingots, coins, church plate, and often religious emblems and jewelry.

SOUTH AMERICA *

Thirty-five Portuguese Naos (unidentied by name) (1)

Thirty-five unidentified Portuguese naos were sunk by pirates in 1572, three miles northeast of Campos off São Joao de Barra, Espirito Santo, Brazil. This combined fleet consisted of approximately $121,000,000 in gold and silver bullion from the rich Sebastian Ferandes Tourinho placer mines in northeastern Brazil, and the crews, rather than surrender their cargoes of treasure, sank them.

Golden Hinde (2)

British frigate, under Sir Francis Drake, after the huge seizure of treasure from the Spanish galleon *Nuestra Señora*

---

* No. 42 describes the submerged city of Coati and an Incan town.

de la Concepción, in order to lighten the frigate, dropped forty-five tons of pure silver, valued at some $20,000,000 at the time, overboard in a cove off the north side of Cano Island (often called La Plata, or Silver Island), in April 1572, in ten fathoms of water. A British salvage syndicate has salvaged some fifteen tons to date.

San Philip II (3)

Spanish galleon sank August 12, 1591, one mile northeast of Flores, in Guanabara Bay, off Neves, Brazil, with a cargo of gold and silver bullion valued at $2,000,000.

Santa Maria (4)

Spanish galleon sank August 12, 1591, one mile northeast of Flores, in Guanabara Bay, off Neves, Brazil, with a cargo valued at $3,500,000 in gold and silver bullion.

Buen Jesus (5)

Spanish galleon sank July 4, 1598, six miles northeast of Portobello, Panama, with $2,000,000 in gold and silver bullion and specie.

Four Spanish Galleons (6)

Fleet of General Luis Hernandez de Cordoba, consisting of the galleons *San Roque, Santa Domingo, San Ambrosio,* and *Nuestra Señora de Begoña,* foundered in 1605, in shallow water, on La Valira shoals off Serrana Bank, 260 miles due east of Point Gorda, Nicaragua, with $4,000,000 in gold bullion, silver and specie.

Unidentified Spanish Galleon (7)

Foundered August 10, 1610, in thirteen fathoms, two miles off Titumate, in Gulf of Uraba, Colombia, with $5,000,000 in ducats, guilders, rix-dollars and church plate seized from a Dutch frigate. The galleon was sunk by pirates.

San Nicholas (8)

Manila galleon foundered in six fathoms, May 13, 1647, at mouth of Penco River, outer harbor of Arica, Chile, swamped by earthquake and deluge eruption, with $1,000,000 in gold ingots and specie.

Unidentified Manila Galleon (9)

Sank November 22, 1648, six miles off Santa Elena, Ecuador, with $13,000,000 in gold and silver bullion.

San Juan De Salvamento (10)

Manila galleon sank December 22, 1655, in five fathoms, one-half mile off Sean Island, Mandregan Bay, Ecuador, with $1,000,000 in gold and silver bullion.

Capitana (11)

Spanish galleon of General Francisco de Sota foundered in 1655, in four fathoms, on Chanduy Reefs, off Point Elena, Ecuador, with $3,500,000 in gold and silver bullion.

Santiago (12)

Manila galleon foundered June 12, 1660, in sixty fathoms, twenty-two miles north of Barranquilla, Colombia, with gold and silver bullion.

Unidentified Spanish Galleon (13)

Sunk July 27, 1666, eleven miles offshore of the southern tip of the Gulf of Paria, on Icacos Point (at Serpent's Mouth), Trinidad, with $500,000 in gold and silver bullion and specie.

Five Spanish Galleons (14)

This small flotilla was sunk by the buccaneer Sir Henry Morgan, on March 2, 1669, four miles off La Ceiba, in Lake Maracaibo, Venezuela, in forty fathoms, with an estimated $1,000,000 in gold and silver bullion and specie.

Rosario (15)

Spanish frigate of Chilean government, foundered November 11, 1675, off Ancua, Chile, on shoals in Chacao Canal, which separates Chiloé Island from the northern mainland. The vessel carried down an estimated gold consignment of $200,000 in specie for back payment of Chilean troops, in seven chests.

Santa Cruz (16)

Manila galleon sank December 16, 1680, in six fathoms, off rocks known as Los Ahorcados, Point Elena, Ecuador, with $13,000,000 in gold, silver plate and 30,000,000 pieces-of-eight. Some recovery made.

Unidentified Manila Galleon (17)

Sank June 30, 1681, in eight fathoms, two miles offshore Santa Clara Reefs, Ecuador, with $400,000 in gold bullion, silver plate, and specie. Many coins are, even to this day, washed ashore after heavy storms.

Santa Teresa (18)

Manila galleon foundered April 3, 1683, on shoals, in fifty-two fathoms, twenty-two miles due north of Barranquilla, Colombia, with $100,000 in gold and silver specie.

San Juan De Dios (19)

Manila galleon foundered in 1684, off beach of Tanque, Chile, with religious ornaments looted from Philippine Islands churches, and $500,000 in gold and silver bullion and church plate.

San Pedro (20)

Spanish galleon sank November 3, 1688, in ten fathoms, in Camana harbor, Camana Bay, Peru, with $1,200,000 in gold and silver bullion, silver plate, and specie. To date, $500,000 has been salvaged by an American salvage syndicate,

Begoña (21)

Spanish frigate, sank September 11, 1695, in five fathoms, two miles off the point of El Concon, Chile, carrying down $200,000 in Chilean gold and silver.

San José (22)

Spanish galleon shattered on rocks of Barú Island, between Isla del Tesoro and Barú peninsula, off Cartagena, Colombia, June 8, 1702. The vessel carried down 6,000,000 pesos in wooden chests and barrels.

Santa Cecilia (23)

Manila galleon sank against rock cliffs, May 11, 1702, in fifteen fathoms, off Morro Vuido, San Fernandez Island, Chile, with a treasure cargo estimated at $5,000,000 in gold bullion and silver plate from the Potosi mines of Peru. Two years later, Alexander Selkirk, a British seaman, who was the real Robinson Crusoe, and who had landed from the *Cinque Ports* galley, spent 1,580 days, from October 1704 to February 1709, on the island, where he wrote his story, published in 1719.

San Josef (24)

A Spanish galleon of sixty-four guns, was sunk, twelve miles northeast by a British man-of-war frigate after leav-

ing Cartagena, Colombia, in 1708. The vessel carried down
nearly $7,000,000 in gold and silver bullion and specie.

Santa Isabel (25)

Manila galleon, sank October 4, 1721, three-quarters
of a mile off the northwestern tip of Santa Clara Island,
Ecuador, in Gulf of Guayaquil, with $700,000 in gold bullion
and silver plate.

Santa Teresa (26)

Manila galleon, sank May 12, 1734, in eleven fathoms,
off the southern side of channel, Puna Island, Ecuador,
with $2,000,000 in gold bullion and silver plate.

Encarnación (27)

Manila galleon, sank in 1702, off Chiloé, Chile, with
approximately $100,000 in gold specie.

San José (28)

Manila galleon, sank June 2, 1763, in fourteen fathoms,
two miles offshore of the western point of Santa Elena,
Ecuador, with $1,800,000 in gold and silver bullion and
plate.

Aurora (29)

Spanish galleon, sank August 17, 1772, in four fathoms,
one-half mile southeast of Piedros de Pedros Rocks, close
to the old site of the powder magazine some six hundred

yards southeast of the rocks, in Montevideo harbor, Uruguay. The treasure was from the Chilean silver mines, and estimated at $2,500,000 in silver plate.

Santissima Concepción (30)

Spanish galleon, foundered November 11, 1775, in twenty-one fathoms, thirty-four miles off the northeastern tip of Margarita Island, just south of Los Frailes, Venezuela. The galleon carried down an estimated treasure cargo of $5,000,000 in gold bullion and silver specie.

Nuestra Señora De La Balbanera (31)

Spanish frigate (payship), foundered on reefs of Guapacho, off San Carlos, Chiloé, Chile, while sailing through narrow channel into the Gulf of Ancud, with a cargo of $200,000 in gold and silver specie. It rests in six fathoms of water. Sank December 23, 1788.

Nine Unidentified Spanish Galleons (32)

Spanish galleons of a fleet of treasure-bearing vessels, sank in 1797, in twelve fathoms, two miles off Chaguaramas, Chaguaramas Island, Trinidad, with $3,000,000 in gold and silver bullion and specie.

Todos Santos (33)

Manila galleon, sank June 3, 1799, off the western end of Guano Islands, eighteen miles due west of Paita, Peru, with $3,500,000 in gold and silver bullion and specie. This vessel was sunk by Thomas Gage (Sieur Raveneau de

Lussan), notorious renegade and pirate of the west coast. To date $20,000 has been salvaged.

Santa Leocadia (34)

Manila frigate foundered November 16, 1800, in fifteen fathoms, on shoals one hundred yards off Point Santa Elena, Ecuador. The vessel was a thirty-four-gun frigate, carrying 2,500,000 pesos in gold and silver, in wooden chests. To date 1,800,000 pesos recovered by salvage, with approximately $250,000 remaining.

Asunción (35)

Manila galleon, dashed to pieces against the rocks of Banco Ingles, Peru, May 20, 1805, in fourteen fathoms. The vessel carried down gold and silver bullion and specie valued at $1,500,000.

San Pedro De Alcántara (36)

Spanish galleon, sank February 24, 1815, in twelve fathoms, five miles due south of western tip of Coche Island, Venezuela. The vessel was one of a fleet under General Pablo Morillo, and carried gold and silver bullion and specie estimated at $5,000,000. Several salvage operations have recovered considerable treasure, while $250,000 in coins have been recovered from the beaches, washed up by storms.

Thetis (37)

British frigate, sank December 4, 1830, in five fathoms, in cave, 1,500 feet off Cape Frio, Espirito Santo Province, Brazil, with $810,000 in gold and silver bullion and specie. In 1831, a British salvage syndicate, with the sloop *Lightning*, recovered $700,000, leaving approximately $110,000 still buried in the seabed within the cave.

Madagascar (38)

British frigate, sank in storm February 29, 1853, in twelve fathoms, one and a half miles off the mouth of the Paranagua River, Brazil, with $3,000,000 (700 pounds) in gold nuggets and dust from the Australian goldfields. Some salvage made.

Sakkarah (39)

German steamer, of the German Kosmos Line, sank April 14, 1902, in eight fathoms, against offshore rocks of Guamblin Island, Chile, with cargo of gold and silver bullion, and nitrates. The nitrates cargo was en route for German munitions manufacturers, and is valued at $67,000; the gold and silver consignment is valued at $350,000.

West Chetac (40)

American steamer was torpedoed off British Guiana, in Latitude 08° 06′ N., longitude 58° 12′ W., September 24, 1942, in thirty fathoms. The vessel carried a cargo of steel, tin, copper, aluminum sheets, and specie of $30,000.

Miscellaneous Treasure Sites (41)

In Cartagena harbor and off Points Canoas, Baru, and the islands of Tierra Bomba and Rosario rest huge caches of treasure, which were lost when numerous Spanish galleons and frigates bearing rich cargoes en route back to Spain were sunk.

Submerged Cities (42)

In Lake Titicaca, Peru, the ancient city of Coati rests below Coati Island. The Incas called the island "Island of the Moon." It was populated by white men who furnished the race of Inca emperors. Monuments, gold and silver ornaments, and artifacts have been fished up from the depths on various occasions.

Off Calloa, Peru, in the Milne-Edward Deep, rests an ancient submerged settlement of an Inca community which was submerged following an earthquake, as Incan legend records.

UNITED KINGDOM *

Norse Galley Serpent (1)

In the year 852, this ancient vessel sank at the entrance to the mouth of the Thames River, off what is today known as the village of Sheerness, Kent county, England.

---

* No. 40 describes the submerged city of Cudlow and an ancient fortress.

As the crew had been pillaging the region, the galley was recorded in early archives as having gold and silver relics and artifacts whose estimated value would probably be in excess of $1,000,000.

Girona (2)

Spanish galleon foundered in 1588, in shallow water, on Bombay Rocks, off Ballintoy, near mouth of Bush River, between Giant's Causeway and Rathlin Island, Ireland, with an estimated $1,000,000 in gold bullion and silver specie.

St. Andrew (3)

A Portuguese galleon payship of the Armada, foundered December 16, 1588, in fourteen fathoms, in Gunwalloe Cove, off Land's End, Cornwall, England. The vessel carried down a treasure in gold and silver bullion and specie amounting to $2,000,000, including eight thousand cakes of copper, eighteen blocks of silver, silver vessels, jewels, four sets of armor for the King of Portugal, and a silver-decorated harness for His Majesty's horses.

Two Unidentified Galleons (4)

Spanish galleons foundered in mid-center of Mount's Bay, Cornwall, England, June 18, 1559, in eleven fathoms, with gold and silver bullion and specie valued at approximately $500,000.

Pereira (5)

Spanish galleon payship of the Armada, sank July 27, 1588, in nine fathoms, offshore between Deal and Ramsgate, Kent county, England, with an estimated gold and silver bullion and specie treasure amounting to $16,000,000.

El Gran Grifon (6)

Spanish galleon payship of the Armada, foundered July 24, 1588, in fourteen fathoms, four miles off Foula, north northeast of the Shetland Islands, Scotland. The vessel carried down $700,000 in gold and silver bullion and specie for troop payment.

Santa Maria De La Rose (7)

Spanish galleon foundered September 21, 1588, in fourteen fathoms, on Stromboli Rock, off east side Begimsh and Young Islands, in Blasket Sound, County Kerry, Ireland, with 50,000 ducats of silver, and as much more in gold bullion and specie. In 1963 an expedition failed to locate the remains; however, in 1967, the site was relocated, and salvage operations are being planned.

El Gran Duque De Florencia (8)

Spanish galleon payship sank November 15, 1588, in fifty fathoms, off McBrain's Landing, Island of Mull, in Mull Sound, Argyle, Scotland, with $8,100,000 in gold and silver bullion and specie. Numerous salvage attempts to

unearth this treasure from the bay's bottom have failed to
date.

Santa Catalina (9)

Spanish galleon payship of the Armada sank July 9,
1588, in twelve fathoms, offshore Collieston, Aberdeen, on
the east coast of Scotland, with gold and silver bullion in
ingots and bars.

Unidentified Galleon Payship (10)

Spanish galleon payship of the Armada sank September 12, 1588, in ten fathoms, at site called St. Catherin's Dub, five miles north of Collieston, Aberdeen, on east
coast of Scotland (two hundred yards offshore). The vessel
carried down gold and silver bullion and specie estimated
at $1,000,000.

Unidentified Galleon Payship (11)

Spanish payship of the Armada sank October 12, 1588,
in shallow water, off Rosses coast, Donegal, Ireland, in
an area called Mullaghderg Strand, near Kincasslagh. The
vessel's treasure consignment is estimated at nearly $2,000,-
000 in gold and silver bullion and specie.

Invincible (12)

Spanish galleon of the Armada sunk by British frigate
July 13, 1588, a payship of the Armada with consignment
of the fleet's pay estimated at six and a half million francs

in silver and gold specie. The vessel was sunk just off Ramsgate, Kent, England.

British Frigate Fleet (13)

In 1651, a fleet of British frigates, under General Monk, captured the city of Dundee, loaded the vessels with treasure estimated at $2,000,000. The entire fleet was sunk in storm off Budden Ness, in the Firth of Tay, off the outer waters of Dundee, Angus, Scotland, in shallow waters.

Santa Cruz (14)

Spanish galleon foundered January 11, 1679, in six fathoms, on rocks offshore Pembroke, West Wales, with $12,000,000 in gold and silver bullion and specie.

Infanta (15)

Spanish galleon sank November 14, 1683, in twenty-one fathoms, offshore Bantry Bay, Cork, Ireland. The vessel carried down 1,100 silver bars in twenty wooden chests, church plate, and gold bullion amounting to nearly $250,000.

El Dorado (16)

Spanish galleon struck rocks off Worms Head, Swansea, South Wales, October 3, 1691, with gold and silver specie amounting to $250,000, in seven fathoms. $40,000 recovered to date.

Little Duck (17)

Spanish galleon sank in nine fathoms, on June 4, 1699, offshore Seaton Carew, Hartlepool, England, with $600,000 in gold and silver bullion and specie. $100,000 salvaged to date.

Association (18)

British frigate of ninety-six guns, under command of Sir Cloudesley Shovel, in four fathoms, October 22, 1707, struck rocks one mile off Bishop Rock, near where Bishop Rock lighthouse now stands, in Outer Gilstone, Scilly Islands. A treasure in gold bullion and silver specie valued at more than $2,000,000 was carried down. The frigate has, on various ocasions, been partially salvaged, but only pewter, vases, and cannon have been recovered to date.

De Liefe (19)

Dutch carrack, shattered against the Mioness Reefs, Shetland Islands, in October 1711. The vessel carried gold and silver specie. Some small salvage has been made.

Unidentified Spanish Galleon (20)

Spanish galleon sank January 17, 1750, in four fathoms, off the rocky cliffs of St. Winawalloe, Cornwall, England, with an estimated treasure in gold and silver bullion and specie loss of $1,380,000.

Unidentified Spanish Galleon (21)

Foundered June 7, 1790, in ten fathoms, off Porten-cross, England, with $300,000 in gold and silver bullion and specie. Some cannon were recovered at the time of loss.

Unidentified Portuguese Galleon (22)

The galleon was sunk by Guernsey pirates, who set fire to the vessel December 12, 1799, offshore Ballinskelligs, Kerry, Ireland. The vessel carried down $700,000 in gold and silver bullion from the Minas Geraes Brazilian mines. The exact site of sinking was in an area known as Waterville.

Guernsey Lily (23)

British frigate sank December 11, 1799, in eight fathoms, at the entrance of Solent, off Yarmouth Roads, Hants, England, with $300,000 in gold and silver bullion and specie. Approximately $150,000 has been recovered to date.

Active (24)

British frigate foundered January 10, 1803, in ten fathoms, in Margate Roads, Kent, England, with $200,000 in specie.

Hindostan (25)

British East India frigate sank January 12, 1803, in six fathoms, on wedge of Margate Spit, off Culvers, Kent, England, with $300,000 in silver specie stowed in thirteen chests. Eleven chests, valued at $40,000, have been salvaged to date.

Earl of Abergavenny (26)

British East India frigate foundered February 16, 1805, in twelve fathoms, two miles offshore Weymouth, Shambles of Portland Bill, Dorset, England, with $700,000 in gold bullion and porcelain. Some salvage has been made.

Anson (27)

British frigate foundered December 8, 1807, in six fathoms, off rocks of Looe Bar, Mount's Bay, Cornwall, England, with $1,200,000 in gold and silver bullion and specie. The vessel was a forty-one-gun man-of-war paymaster ship of the British Fleet in the Atlantic at the time.

Susan and Rebecca (28)

British frigate sank November 4, 1807, in four fathoms, off the cliffs of Hal-Zephron, Gunwalloe Cove, Cornwall, England, with a treasure cargo estimated at $300,000 in gold and silver specie.

Jenny (29)

British frigate foundered December 28, 1809, against rock cliffs near cave mouth, on Lundy Island, in British Channel, in four fathoms, with consignment of gold specie, silver bars, and ivory, valued at $1,000,000.

Unidentified "Silver Ship" (30)

An unidentified Dutch frigate foundered in 1821, on reefs near Heilinabretta, Fetlar, Shetland Islands, with an estimated treasure of some $300,000. Even to this day, great quantities of Dutch coins are washed up on the Heilinabretta shores.

Royal Charter (31)

British steamer of 119 tons, foundered October 26, 1859, in four fathoms, on offshore rocks off Red Wharf Bay, Lynas Head, Wales, with $1,750,000 in silver bullion and ivory. To date $1,300,000 has been salvaged.

Crescent City (32)

British steamer sank November 14, 1869, in sixteen fathoms, offshore Galley Head, South Cork, Ireland, with $250,000 in gold specie. To date $55,000 has been salvaged.

Port Yarrock (33)

British steamer sank in 1894, in eleven fathoms, on reefs in Brandon Bay, Kerry, Ireland, with $400,000 in gold and silver specie and copper.

Oceana (34)

British steamer sank March 16, 1912, in thirteen fathoms, two miles off Royal Sovereign Lightship, Beachy Head, Sussex, England, with $3,000,000 in gold bullion and silver specie. In 1912, the Liverpool Salvage Association recovered approximately $2,500,000.

Hampshire (35)

British cruiser torpedoed June 5, 1916, off Marwick Head, between Brough of Birdsay and Marwich Head, west coast of Orkney Islands, Scotland. The cruiser rests in forty fathoms, and carried $9,260,000 in British gold sovereigns and specie. England's most famous soldier-statesman, Lord Kitchener, was lost aboard the vessel. Only $60,000 has been recovered to date.

Laurentic (36)

British steamer torpedoed January 25, 1917, in twenty fathoms, fifteen miles off the mouth of Lough Swilly, Donegal, Ireland. The steamer carried $25,000,000 in 3,211 gold ingots, meant for payment to the United States for munitions purchased. The Malet Salvage Syndicate, Ltd. recovered 3,051 ingots from the sunken White Star liner, valued today at $24,650,000

Lusitania (37)

British steamer torpedoed May 7, 1917, in fifty fathoms, eight miles off Old Head of Kinsale, South Cork, Ireland. The vessel carried $800,000 in gold bullion, three safes of jewels and specie of the passengers. (These figures are substantiated by confidential records in the United States State Department.) Latest reports are that this vessel is about to be salvaged.

Argonaut (38)

American steamer sunk June 5, 1918, in sixty-five fathoms, by German submarine in English Channel, south of Land's End, Cornwall, England (Latitude 49° 12' N., Longitude 6° 45' W.). The steamer carried approximately $300,000 in gold and silver bullion and specie.

Empress of Britain (39)

British steamer sank October 1940, offshore Bloody Floorland, England, with 50,000,000 French francs.

Submerged Cities (40)

A submerged village, at the time called Cudlow, sank in the seventeenth century, at the mouth of the Arun River, off Littlehampton, Sussex, England. Relics and artifacts may still be recovered.

An ancient fortress rests at the bottom of the channel off Sclooy Bill, Sussex, England, approximately one mile offshore. In the seventeenth century, the site was flooded by a terrific current of the sea. Relics and artifacts of the ruins and stone walls used as catapult ammunition stores may still be recovered.

EUROPE °

119 Unidentified Greek Triemes (1)

Foundered in 413 B.C., in sixty fathoms, off Ortigia Island, Siracusa Bay, Sicily, Italy, with gold and silver ornaments, statues, and amphorae, This loss was known as the "Fleet of Disasters," under command of the Athenian general Alcibides, who had led his fleet of 134 warships against the Corinthian colony of Syracuse, Greece's greatest colonial possession 2,781 years ago.

Seven Unidentified Greek Galleys (2)

Foundered in 641, in shallow water, off Flat Island (ancient name of Yassi Ada), in Chuka Channel, treasure-laden.

° No. 40 describes the ancient submerged city of Epidarus, the submerged city of Kenchreai, the Temple of Hera Lacinia, and two other submerged villages.

Six Unidentified Danish Galleys (3)

Foundered in 1361, in forty fathoms, twelve miles off the northeastern tip of Oland Island, on the eastern Boda Reefs, Gotland, Sweden, with gold, silver, artifacts, and amphorae.

Four Unidentified Greek Galleys (4)

Foundered in 1472, in forty-two fathoms, midway between Kithira (Cerigo) and Andikithia Island, Greece, with an estimated $4,000,000 in gold and silver ornaments, statues, and amphorae.

Three Unidentified Greek Galleys (5)

Foundered in 1472, in shallow water, off Iraklion, Crete, Sea of Crete, close to (Cerigo), with 14,000,000 francs in value. These were slave boats.

Unidentified Roman Galley (6)

Foundered in 1491, in nineteen fathoms, one and a half miles off Kithira (Cerigo) Island, Greece, with an estimated $7,000,000 in gold and silver ornaments, statues, and amphorae.

Unidentified Greek Galley (7)

Foundered March 12, 1501, in eleven fathoms, two miles off Ancona, in Adriatic Sea, Italy, with an estimated

$2,000,000 in gold and silver ornaments, statues, and amphorao.

Unidentified Greek Galley (8)

Foundered April 3, 1501, in twenty-eight fathoms, just off Ancona, in Adriatic Sea, with 7,000,000 francs.

Five Unidentified Greek Galleys (9)

Foundered in 1502, in shallow waters, two miles off Koca Point, in Bodrum Bay, Turkey, with unknown amount of gold specie, bronze and gold statuary and ornaments, in twelve to twenty fathoms.

Jean Florin (10)

French corsair foundered December 12, 1522, off Les Minquiers, north northeast of France, with an estimated $850,000 in gold and silver bullion, and the historical gold wardrobe of Montezuma, the Aztec Emperor.

Isabela (11)

Spanish galleon foundered June 4, 1672, in ten fathoms, five miles off the southern shore of Cape Maria, Spain, with $750,000 in gold and silver bullion and specie.

Cardia (12)

Greek galley sank June 3, 1686, in seventeen fathoms, two miles east of Ancona, in Adriatic Sea, with an estimated $1,500,000 in gold and silver statues and amphorae.

Fourteen Spanish Galleons (13)

Foundered September 2, 1702, in approximately forty fathoms, one mile northwest of Los Castros de Agoziro, Rande, Vigo Bay, Spain, with an estimated $140,000,000 in gold and silver bullion and plate. The vessels were the *Santissima Trinidad, Jesus Maria Joseph, San Juan Baptista, Santo Cristo de Maracaja, Santo Cristo de Buen Viaje, La Santa Cruz, Santo Domingo, El Toro (Santa Susana), San Diego, La Sacra Familia, Felipe Quinto, Nuestra Señora de las Animas, Nuestra Señora de del Rosario, Nuestra Señora da las Mercedes, Nuestra Señora de los Dolores, Nuestra Señora de las Angustias,* and *Jesus Maria José y las Animas.* Numerous salvage attempts have been made to recover this wealth, but few have retrieved very much.

Santa Teresa (14)

Spanish galleon, foundered February 4, 1704, in six fathoms, off Tagus Bar, near Lisbon, with $500,000 in gold and silver.

Unidentified Dutch Frigate (15)

Foundered in 1767, twenty-one miles offshore of Sheveling, Shoals of Texal, Holland, with $6,000,000 in gold and silver bullion, plate and specie.

General Barker (16)

British frigate foundered February 17, 1781, in six fathoms, on reefs of the Dutch Shoals, Holland, with

$4,000,000 in gold bullion and specie. To date $1,000,000 has been salvaged.

San Pedro De Alcantára (17)

Spanish galleon foundered January 17, 1786, in twenty-one fathoms, one and a half miles off Estremadura, northwest Portugal, with $800,000 in gold and silver bullion, and 8,000,000 pieces-of-eight. To date $400,000 has been salvaged.

Hartwell (18)

British frigate sank May 6, 1787, in two fathoms, two miles off Cape Verde Islands, Portugal, with an estimated $2,000,000 in gold bullion.

Quintanadoine-Telemaque (19)

French barque foundered January 3, 1790, in thirty fathoms, off Quillebeauf, at the mouth of the Seine River, France, with an estimated $20,000,000 in gold and silver bullion, specie and statues, including the $5,000,000 *riviere* of Queen Marie Antoinette. Salvage attempts have failed to recover any substantial amount of the treasure to date.

Conqueror (20)

British frigate foundered in 1791, off Point Saint Quentin, in Tourmont (Bay of Somme), at mouth of Somme River, in English Channel, with 3,000,000 francs.

Lutine (21)

British frigate foundered October 9, 1799, in twenty fathoms, off Fly Island, between Vlieland and Terschelling, Holland, with $4,650,000 in gold and silver bullion, specie, inclusive of $812,000 gold specie, and 564 gold ingots. To date some $850,000 has been recovered, and the famous "Lutine Bell" and other relics are on display in Lloyd's of London. Numerous salvage attempts have been made to recover this wealth, but few have been successful.

Cantabria (22)

Spanish corvette foundered May 12, 1802, off Cadiz, Spain, in latitude 27° N., longitude 28° W. The vessel carried down $1,000,000 in gold and silver bullion, and gems.

Mercedes (23)

Spanish frigate foundered October 5, 1804, in deep water, thirty miles SW of Cape Santa Maria, Spain (latitude 36° 26′ N., longitude 8° 10′ W.), with $1,000,000 in gold and silver bullion, and specie. The vessel was commanded by José Hustamante.

Unidentified French Corsair (24)

Foundered December 6, 1806, in two fathoms, two miles off Port-Saint Louis, at the mouth of the Rhone River, France, with $1,300,000 in gold and silver bullion, statues, and Napoleonic era antiques and ornaments.

Unidentified French Corsair (25)

Foundered December 6, 1806, in six fathoms, at Rhone River Estuary, France, with 4,000,000 francs.

Polluce (formerly *Luce*) (26)

Spanish galleon foundered October 29, 1806, in forty-five fathoms, one and a half miles off Porto Longo (Livorno), Leghorn, Italy, with $1,200,000 in gold and silver church plate.

Le Jeune Henri (27)

French schooner foundered December 8, 1820, in six fathoms, midway between Charantes River and Oleron Island, France, with $3,000,000 in gold, silver, and jewels in eleven chests.

129 Unidentified Turkish Frigates and Fireships (28)

Foundered October 20, 1827, in thirty-two fathoms, off Pilos, Peloponnesus Island, Navarina Bay, Greece, with an estimated loss of $70,000,000 in gold and silver bullion and specie. These craft were sunk during the Battle of Navarino Bay, the last battle of the wooden navies.

Captain Bey (29)

Foundered October 20, 1827, in twenty-seven fathoms, off Pilos, Peloponnesus Island, Navarino Bay, Greece, with an estimated loss in gold and silver bullion and specie of $16,000,000, in tho Turkiah admiral'a flagship.

Guerriene (30)

Egyptian frigate, flagship of the Egyptian admiral, foundered October 20, 1827, in thirty-six fathoms, off Pilos, Peloponnesus Island, Navarino Bay, Greece, with an estimated loss of $10,000,000 in gold and silver bullion and specie.

Ville De Grasse (31)

French paddlewheel steamer sank in 1851, in shallow water, just off Por Querolles Island, between Toulon and Nice, France, with $100,000 in Luis de 'Or specie.

Black Prince (32)

British steamer foundered November 12, 1854, off Sebastapol, Balaclava Bay, in Black Sea, with an estimated $5,000,000 in gold bullion, a consignment to the Bank of England, 2,700 tons of which was insured by Lloyd's of London for $2,000,000. Russian, English, and Japanese salvage attempts, just prior to World War I, sought the wreck without success. However, after the Soviet Union failed in their operation, it was rumored falsely that the consignment had been unloaded at Istanbul, Turkey, but this report was unsubstantiated.

Skyro (33)

British steamer foundered in 1891, in twenty-eight fathoms, three miles off Mexiddo Reef, nine miles from Cape Finisterre, France, with $200,000 in gold and silver bullion and specie. To date $50,000 has been salvaged.

Drummond Castle (34)

British steamer foundered in 1897, in thirty-three fathoms, on the Pierres Vertes rocks, one-half mile off Molene Island, in Frombeur Channel, France, with $400,-000 in gold bullion.

Tubantia (35)

Dutch steamer foundered March 10, 1916, in twenty-seven fathoms, two miles east off the North Hinder Lightship, Hinder Bank, North Sea, with $1,500,000 in gold bullion hidden in Dutch cheeses. The vessel was torpedoed by a German submarine. To date $100,000 has been recovered.

Renate Leonhardt (36)

German steamer foundered in 1917, in eleven fathoms, twelve miles off Zaandam harbor, Holland, with $2,000,000 in gold and silver bullion in 454 chests.

Elizabethville (37)

Belgian steamer foundered September, 1917, in forty fathoms, one-half mile off the southern point of Belle Isle, near Quiberon Point, France, with $2,500,000 in gold and silver bullion and specie, ivory and diamonds. To date $500,000 in ivory and four chests of gold and silver have been salvaged.

Egypt (38)

British steamer foundered May 20, 1922, in sixty-five fathoms, with $6,200,000 in gold and silver bullion and specie, one mile off Hedbeck's Point, Biscay Bay, France. To date $5,000,000 has been recovered by a salvage company.

Swedish and Danish Wrecks (39)

The Swedish and Danish waters hold large numbers of treasure-bearing wrecks spread over a period from early Viking times (A.D. 1000) down to the present. Salvage of such treasure-carrying wrecks as the British frigates *Defense* and *St. George* (1811), the Dutch frigate *Brederode* (1658), the Russian steamer *Alexandr Nevski* (1868), and numerous others still unsalvaged off North and West Zeeland and Jutland requires the permission for exploratory operations from the Swedish and Danish Antiquity authorities.

Sunken Cities (40)

The ancient city of Epidaurus sank in the year 250 A.D., and now rests in ten fathoms, in St. Ivan's Bay, two miles off Cavat Cragusa Vecchia, seven miles southeast of Dubrovnik, in the Adriatic Sea. This site is in Montenegro Province, Yugoslavia. Gold and slver ornaments, works of metal art, statues, pottery, and amphorae can still be salvaged.

The submerged city of Kenchreai, off Greece, was inundated approximately 1,500 years ago by the sea. The ancient relics and artifacts of the Temple of Isis, dwellings, church, and warehouse in the harbor are still well-preserved to this day, and can be explored.

Another submerged city's relics and artifacts are still existent offshore of the village of Crotone, a small fishing village. The fabulous temple in Calabria Province, Italy of Hera Lacinia, and other objects, including gold and silver artifacts and amphorae, are located beneath the surface waters.

In Lake Bolsema, approximately sixty miles north of Rome, Italy, a submerged community still exists for exploration.

In Pilakno Lake, near Mragowo, Poland, rests the submerged remains of a city which sank in 500 B.C.

AFRICA

São Bento (1)

Portuguese nao foundered June 3, 1554, in about thirty-two fathoms, just off the mouth of Umzimvubu River, near Port Saint Johns, Transke, southeast Africa, with an estimated $1,000,000 in gold, silver and gems, now buried deep in sand.

Garca (2)

Portuguese nao foundered November 4, 1559, in approximately thirty-four fathoms, two miles off Vila de Joao Belo, off mouth of Limpopo River, Mozambique, southeast Africa, with chests of gold valued at $500,000.

Portuguese Carrack (3)

Foundered July 12, 1580, in eighty fathoms, in False Bay, near Cape Town, South Africa, with $250,000 in silver bullion and specie.

Unidentified Portuguese Carrack (4)

Foundered June 4, 1584, in False Bay, off Cape Town, South Africa, with $100,000 in silver specie and some plate.

Santiago (5)

Portuguese carrack foundered August 19, 1585, in twenty fathoms, on reefs on the southern edge of Bassas de India atoll, halfway between Safala and Cape Saint Vincent, Madagascar, with gold and silver valued at $300,000.

Saint James (6)

Portuguese galleon foundered September 16, 1586, in nine fathoms, in False Bay, off Galedon, just south of Cape

Town, South Africa, with gold and silver amounting to $500,000.

San Goncalo (7)

Portuguese galleon sank September 12, 1630, in fifty-eight fathoms, off Bahia Fermoza, near Cape Seal (Plattenberg Bay area), South Africa, with $2,000,000 in silver plate.

Sacramento (8)

Portuguese carrack broke up in Algoa Bay, just off Port Elizabeth, South Africa, in seven fathoms, July 19, 1647, with $1,000,000 in gold and silver, and slaves, buried under sand.

Haarlem II (9)

Dutch frigate foundered March 12, 1648, in four fathoms, off mouth of Salt River (off Woodstock Beach), South Africa, with gold and silver bullion and specie valued at the time at $2,500,000, buried in a sand bottom.

Unidentified Dutch Frigate (10)

Foundered April 12, 1693, in fifteen fathoms, 35 miles south southeast of Nosy Angontsy Island, Madagascar (latitude 15° 16′, longitude 50° 29′), with $500,000 in gold and silver bullion.

Madre De Deus (11)

Spanish galleon foundered June 9, 1594, in five fathoms, off Ras Asir (Cape Guardafui), Somali Republic, with gold and silver bullion and jewels valued at $500,000.

Unidentified Dutch Frigate (12)

Foundered April 12, 1693, in fifteen fathoms, two and a half miles northeast off Teneriffe Island, Canary Islands, with $500,000 in gold and silver bullion.

Dageraad (13)

Dutch frigate foundered March 14, 1694, in ten fathoms, one mile off the west side of Robben Island, South Africa, with $1,300,000 in gold and silver bullion and specie. After heavy storms, considerable numbers of coins are still washed ashore.

Het Huis Te Crayenstein (14)

Dutch frigate foundered February 11, 1698, in ten fathoms, three miles off Camps Bay, on rocks near Oudekrall, South Africa. The vessel carried $1,300,000 in gold and silver bullion and specie in nineteen chests. Two chests have been recovered, the others still buried deep in the sand.

Two Unidentified Dutch Frigates (15)

Foundered between 1700-1716, in from twelve to twenty fathoms, off Milnerton, Table Bay, South Africa, carrying down an estimated $3,000,000 in gold and silver bullion, specie, and porcelain.

Forty-Two Unidentified Dutch Frigates (16)

Between the years 1704 and 1720, forty-two unidentified Dutch frigates, treasure-laden, sank in twenty fathoms of water, in Table Bay, South Africa, carrying down an estimated $100,000,000 in gold and silver bullion, porcelain, specie, and other unperishable treasure.

Meresteyn (17)

Dutch frigate foundered April 3, 1702, in fourteen fathoms, off the southwest side of Jutten Island, South Africa, with consignment of $1,000,000 from the Bank of Amsterdam for Cape Town bankers, in silver.

Unidentified Spanish Galleon (18)

Foundered June 4, 1736, one mile off Sandwich Harbor, South Africa, with $3,000,000 consignment in gold and silver bullion, specie, porcelain and other treasure, in fourteen fathoms.

Yonge Thomas (19)

Dutch frigate foundered June 2, 1775, in twelve fathoms, off Milnerton, Table Bay, South Africa, with $800,000 in gold bullion and specie.

La Gloire (20)

French frigate wrecked June 2, 1775, in twelve fathoms, four miles off Nosy Antontsy Island, Madagascar (latitude 15° 54' S., longitude 50° 14' E.), with $100,000 in gold specie.

San Vicente (21)

Spanish galleon foundered February 2, 1780, in four fathoms, off Port d'Ilheo, Sandwich Harbor, South Africa, with $2,000,000 in gold and silver bullion and specie.

Middleburg (22)

Dutch frigate foundered June 10, 1781, in twenty fathoms, two miles off Meeuw Island, South Africa, with $200,000 in gold specie.

Grosvenor (23)

British frigate foundered in Lady's Bay (the Transki), East Africa, August 4, 1782, in eight fathoms, carrying down $15,360,000 in gold and silver bullion and diamonds. The cargo in treasure consisted of two thousand ingots of silver; 720 ingots of gold, diamonds, emeralds, and other jewels;

two gem-encrusted golden peacocks from the throne of the Great Mogul, Emperor Shahjehan, builder of the Taj Mahal, who erected the "peacock" throne in 1605 at a cost of $15,000,000; it was later filched by a Persian invader in 1739, Nadir Shah, from Delhi, India. Numerous salvage efforts have taken place on this wreck. The latest was in 1952, when salvors recovered close to $1,000,000 worth of gold and silver, but did not return to England, their homeland, due to taxation, and are now residing in Brazil.

Winterton (24)

British frigate dashed to pieces on rocky shoals in 1792, in six fathoms, six miles off Baie de Saint Augustin, near Tulear, Madagascar, with $800,000 in gold, silver and jewels.

L'Orient (25)

French frigate sank August 2, 1798, after crashing against the reefs between Culloden's Reef and Aboukir Island, in Aboukir Bay, Egypt. The vessel carried down some $5,500,-000 in gold bullion, silver and specie; artifacts, including the historical original religious ornaments of the Knights of Malta (Crusaders), which had been filched from the Church of St. John's at Valetta; plus $2,000,000 in solid silver castings of the Twelve Apostles, the silver doors from the Malta Cathedral, and gold and silver jewels seized in Malta by Napoleon. In 1950, King Farouk of Egypt, financed an expedition to retrieve this treasure, but located only a few tons of copper, cast iron and lead, and some specie.

Glot Ter Hooge (26)

Dutch frigate sank in 1799, in twelve fathoms, twenty miles north off Porto Santo, Madeira Islands, with $500,000 in gold, silver, and specie.

Unidentified Spanish Galleon (27)

Foundered April 27, 1802, in eight fathoms, off southern tip Porto Santo, Madeira Islands, with $1,500,000 in gold and silver bullion and specie.

Athienne (28)

British frigate sank October 27, 1806, in ten fathoms, one and a half miles off Esquerques rocks, Tunisia, with $3,500,-000 consignment in gold and silver bullion and specie.

Birkenhead (29)

British steamer foundered February 25, 1852, in twelve fathoms, on rocks one mile from Danger Point Lighthouse, near Gansbaal, South Africa, with consignment of $5,000-000 in gold sovereigns. The vessel was an iron-clad paddle-wheel steamer. To date some $1,500,000 in gold sovereigns have been recovered by a salvage syndicate. However, coins still are washed ashore after each storm.

Unidentified Dutch Frigate (30)

Foundered in 1868, four miles south of Camp's Bay, South Africa, with considerable treasure (exact amount is unknown).

Gambia (31)

British steamer sank July 9, 1878, in ten fathoms, four miles off the southern tip of Las Palmas, Grand Canary Island, with $1,500,000 in gold and silver and ivory.

Star of Africa (32)

British bark foundered in 1880, in ten fathoms, off Cape Province, on Albatross Rocks, in Simon's Bay, South Africa, with $100,000 in gold and silver specie and gems.

Alphonso XII (33)

Spanish mail steamer foundered November 4, 1885, in twenty-six fathoms, two miles off Point Gando, Canary Islands, with $450,000 in gold and silver bullion and specie. Nine chests recovered, worth $325,000, together with some twenty-five peseta, leaving one chest unsalvaged to date.

Dorothea (34)

British barkentine sank December 17, 1898, in four fathoms, foundered on reefs approximately 150 yards off-shore of Cape Saint Lucia, Zuzuland, East Africa. The vessel carried down approximately $3,500,000 in gold bullion and diamonds, and is buried deep in sand in sheltered lee of the reef.

Tantallon (35)

British steamer foundered in 1901, in ten fathoms, on reef off Robben Island, South Africa, with $200,000 in silver ingots and specie.

Glenartney (36)

British steamer foundered February 12, 1918, in thirty-seven fathoms, just offshore Ile Zembra, off Cape Bon, Tunisia, with $30,000 in gold and silver specie and six thousand tons of tungsten and "streit," a most strategic and valuable metal.

Hypatia (37)

British steamer foundered October 29, 1929, in forty fathoms, off Whale Rock, five miles off Table Bay, South Africa. The vessel carried down $225,000 in copper ingots and chrome ore. To date $140,000 in copper ingots have been salvaged.

Georges Philippar (38)

French steamer foundered May 16, 1932, in thirty-two fathoms, off the northeastern tip of Cape Guardafui, at extreme eastern end of Gulf of Aden, Somaliland Republic, with $180,000 in gold specie and some silver plate.

Miscellaneous (30)

The region known as the "Sunken Graveyard of South Africa," along the five islands of Jutten, Marcus, Malagas, Meeuw, and Schapen, holds untold numbers of unrecorded treasure-bearing Dutch frigate sinkings, and the time-worn V. O. C. coins (the mark of the Dutch East India Company) are washed ashore from time to time by the treacherous waters after storms on these and the surronuding little pieces of land.

ASIA*

Fourteen Mongolian Junks (1)

Unidentified junks sank June 11, 1274, three miles off the northeastern tip of Hakozaki, Japan, in nine fathoms, during battle at the time Genghis Khan's hordes attempted an invasion of what is today known as Japan, carrying down $11,000,000 in gold, silver, and ornaments which had been looted from the island's settlements.

Nine Mongolian Junks (2)

Unidentified junks foundered in storm on October 14, 1281, in thirty fathoms, six miles off Tanshui, at extreme end of Formosa Island, in Tanshui Bay, with an estimated $500,000 in gold and silver ornaments.

---

* No. 29 describes the submerged city of Pahang and the sites of Sodom and Gomorrah.

Fifty-two Mongolian Junks (3)

Unidentified junks foundered September 3, 1278, in twelve fathoms, one mile off Izmir, in harbor, Asiatic Turkey, with an estimated $16,000 in gold and silver ornaments and statuary.

São Paulo (4)

Portuguese nao foundered January 22, 1561, near village of Sasak, Sumatra, with $150,000 in gold and silver specie.

Two Unidentified Japanese Junks (5)

Foundered May 12, 1572, in fifty-two fathoms, off Teshio, Northern Japan, with an estimated $5,000,000 in gold bullion, silver, and specie.

Madre De Dios (6)

Portuguese naos foundered December 4, 1612, in forty-one fathoms, one mile off tip of Kyushu, Kava Island, near Nagasaki, Japan, during a ten-hour battle with two thousand Nippon warriors who fired the galleon's magazine. The vessel carried down $500,000 in gold and silver bullion and specie.

Santo Christo De Burgos (7)

Manila galleon foundered May 12, 1693, in seventeen fathoms, just offshore Tico Island, east of Luzon, Philippine Islands. The vessel carried down $1,000,000 in gold and silver bullion, ivory and gems in iron-bound chests.

San Christo (8)

Manila galleon foundered June 3, 1735, in eight fathoms, six miles north of Capul Island, on the Calentas Reefs, near Luzon, Philippine Islands, with $1,500,000 in gold and silver bullion, specie, silver plate and 60,000 ryalls and pieces-of-eight.

Cabalava (9)

British frigate of 1,200 tons foundered after striking against rocks on the Cargados Garrados Reef, in Indian Ocean, July 7, 1818, in eight fathoms, with $400,000 in Spanish silver pesos.

Unidentified Turkish Cruiser (10)

Foundered June 24, 1824, in five fathoms, just off the mouth of Acre harbor, near Haifa, Israel, with amphorae treasure.

Malabar (11)

British steamer sank February 28, 1860, in eleven fathoms, two miles offshore the mouth of the Gin Ganga River, near the port of Galle, at the southwestern tip of Ceylon, in Indian Ocean, with $450,000 in silver bullion in pesos. To date $150,000 has been salvaged.

Phantom (12)

American ship foundered September 24, 1862, on the Tankan Shan Reefs, off Hongkong, China, with $10,000,000 in gold and silver bullion and ingots from the Mother Lode of California.

George Sand (13)

German bark foundered January 30, 1863, in sixty fathoms, on the Pratas Reefs, approximately 180 miles southwest of Hongkong, China, with $13,000,000 in California gold and silver bullion, and specie from the California Mother Lode.

Libelle (14)

French bark foundered March 4, 1866, on offshore rocks of Wake Island, South Pacific, approximately one mile distant. The vessel carried down $300,000 in gold bullion, silver specie, and quicksilver.

Thunderer (15)

British steamer foundered November 1, 1867, in shallow water, off the mouth of the Hooghly River, near Calcutta, India, with $1,500,000 in California gold bullion and ingots.

Hayamaru-Go (16)

Japanese steamer, 810 tons, foundered March 15, 1868, on reef off Kuruhamas Beach, southwest of Tokyo, Japan, with gold nuggets belonging to Dutch trading company, bronze from Northern Japan, $60,000 worth of Mexican silver, estimated at $500,000, and insured by Lloyd's of London for nearly one billion dollars.

Hamilla Mitchell (17)

British steamer sank in 1869, near Leuconna Reef, off Shanghai, China, with approximately $2,500,000 in Mexican silver dollars. Several salvage operations have been worked on this vessel, until all but about $200,000 remains.

Oneida (18)

American gunboat sank January 24, 1870, in six fathoms, colliding with British steamer *Bombay* fifteen miles north northeast of Yokohama, in Tokyo Bay, Japan, with $400,000 in gold bullion and specie. Some salvage has been made on this vessel, but it has not been completed.

Nina (19)

British ship, formerly *Christina*, foundered July 16, 1873, in twelve fathoms, nine miles north northeast off Hongkong, China. The vessel carried down $500,000 in silver bullion and specie. In 1935, a Chinese fisherman salvaged the vessel's chain cable, chronometer, and some silver ingots valued at $150,000.

Japan (20)

American steamer sunk by fire December 17, 1875, in sixteen fathoms, twelve miles offshore Swatow (Shant 'ow), in Haimen Bay, China, with $1,500,000 in gold and silver bullion. To date $300,000 has been salvaged.

Hanoi (21)

Chinese cruiser foundered June 6, 1894, in forty-nine fathoms, in mid-center of the Gulf of Po Hai (Chihli), China, with $300,000 in silver bullion and specie.

Tak Kwong (22)

Chinese junk foundered May 11, 1905, twenty-two miles east off Denpassar, Bali Straits, Melassian Peninsula, with $200,000 in Chinese gold and silver, and some specie.

Knyaz Surorov (23)

Russian cruiser sunk by Japanese during Russo-Japanese War, February 28, 1905, twelve miles off Tsushima, Tsushima Straits, Sea of Japan. The cruiser was a payship of the Russian Naval Fleet, and carried $1,200,000 in British gold sovereigns.

Admiral Nakimov (24)

Russian cruiser sunk during Russo-Japanese War, May 28, 1905, in fifty fathoms, between islands of Kyushu and Tsushima, in Japan Sea, with $92,750,000 in British gold sovereigns furnished by the Banque de Paris for payment of the Russian Fleet. The vessel was 7,782 tons, under Captain Ruitoff, and was sunk by two Japanese destroyers. In 1938, the Japanese Deep Diving Research Institute sought the pride of the Russians, and again, in 1955, the Pacific Far East Salvage Co. made underwater searches, each without success. This is the richest treasure cache in the waters of the Orient.

Imperator Alexandr (25)

Russian cruiser payship of the Russian Naval Fleet was sunk by Japanese during Russo-Japanese War, May 29, 1905, in forty fathoms, off Tsushima, Tsushima Straits, Sea of Japan, with $500,000 in British gold sovereigns.

Admiral Rozdestvan (26)

Russian cruiser payship sunk by Japanese during Russo-Japanese War, May 29, 1905, off Tsushima, Tsushima Straits, Japan, with $1,000,000 British gold sovereigns.

Thistlegorm (27)

British steamer foundered October 6, 1941, in seventeen fathoms, off extreme entrance to the mouth of the Red Sea, in Strait of Gubal, Gulf of Suez, with $300,000 in gold and silver bullion and specie, and fourteen locomotives.

Seljuk (28)

Turkish steamer of 1,250 tons, under command of Captain Selim Kucuk, sunk June 12, 1917, by French cruiser

Saint Brieux, in five fathoms, in lagoon ten miles north of entrance to Tiran Straits, 110 miles south of Aquaba. The cargo consisted of fifty ammunition cases of gold specie, 130 cases of silver specie, and 820 bars of British gold and silver, valued at $2,000,000. In 1943 and 1952 various attempts of salvage were made without success due to the bottom conditions.

Sunken Cities (29)

The lost city of Pahang sank in the early fourteenth century, in Lake Chini, forty miles up the Pahang River, in a virtually unexplored stretch of water in southeastern Malaya. It was founded by the Siamese, and rests beneath shallow waters, still retaining its relics and artifacts.

The remains of the two biblical cities of Sodom and Gomorrah, swept into the Dead Sea, between Jordan and Israel, by earthquake, and engulfed by the waters of the plains behind them, rest in a two-mile-long stretch of levee which connected the two cities. One of these ruins rests in the Lisan Peninsula Bay waters; the other lies due west of the northern point of the same peninsula, in a rock levee approximately twelve to fifteen feet wide and ten feet rising above the sea-level floor.

AUSTRALIA AND NEW ZEALAND

Batavia (1)

Dutch frigate foundered June 4, 1629, in eleven fathoms, off west side Houtman Abrolhos Reefs, near Geraldton, Western Australia, with $500,000 in silver specie, gold, rubies, sapphires, diamonds, and gem-encrusted statue of Hindu god Siva, in eleven chests.

De Vergulde Draeck (Gilt Dragon) (2)

Dutch frigate foundered October 28, 1655, in ten fathoms, one-half mile offshore Lancelin Island, off ledge at mouth of the Moore River, Western Australia, with $300,000 in gold and silver bullion, plus eight chests of Dutch guilders. It has been reported that some salvage has been made.

Zuydorp (3)

Dutch frigate foundered June 11, 1712, in six fathoms, one and a half miles off Ajana, forty miles north of mouth of Murchison River, five hundred miles north of Perth, Western Australia, with $100,000 in silver specie. A diver, Allan Robinson, of Perth, Australia, is reported to have salvaged some silver coins in 1968.

Unidentified Galleon (4)

Spanish galleon foundered off Boot Reef, East Murray Island, in Torres Strait, North Queensland, September 11, 1702, in ten fathoms, with approximately $2,500,000 in gold and silver bullion and specie.

Aatekerke (5)

Dutch frigate foundered one mile off beach at Perth, Australia, with $500,000 in gold and silver bullion and specie, in 1720.

Eliza (6)

American brig foundered September 12, 1808, in two fathoms, just off the south side of Nairai Island, Fiji Islands, New Zealand, with $40,000 in silver Spanish pesos.

Hope (7)

British frigate foundered April 29, 1827, in six fathoms, two miles off the northern tip of Betsy Island, Tasmania, with $300,000 in gold specie, funds for back payment of the troops stationed in Hobart Town.

Portland (8)

British bark foundered in 1833, in twelve fathoms, on the northern coast of Tasmania, just east of Hebe Reef, off Hobart Town, with $100,000 in gold and silver specie.

Neva (9)

British frigate foundered May 13, 1835, in six fathoms, one mile northeast off King Island, Tasmania, with approximately $100,000 in gold specie.

Enchantress (10)

British bark of 376 tons, foundered July 17, 1835, in eight fathoms, six miles off Bruni Island, off Hobart, Australia, with $200,000 in gold and silver specie.

Lancer (11)

British bark foundered September 22, 1839, in seven fathoms, off Rottnest Rocks, Rottnest Island, near Freemantle, Western Australia, with 7,000 gold sovereigns and $35,000 in silver specie, in seventeen chests.

Britomart (12)

British bark foundered June 3, 1840, in thirteen fathoms, two miles off Preservation Island, Tasmania, with $600,000 in gold and silver bullion and specie.

Catarqui (13)

British frigate foundered August 4, 1845, in ten fathoms, one mile off the northern tip of King Island, Tasmania, with $250,000 in gold specie.

Water Witch (14)

British steamer foundered August 13, 1855, in fifteen fathoms, three miles south southeast off King Island, Tasmania, with consignment of $2,000,000 in gold ingots, nuggets, and dust from the Ballaret Australian Mines.

Catherine Shearer (15)

British frigate foundered July 21, 1855, in eight fathoms, off Port Esperance, Tasmania, with $1,000,000 in gold bullion and specie.

Duncan Dunbar (16)

British ship foundered August 20, 1857, in five fathoms, two miles off Sydney Gap, near Sydney Head Light, New South Wales, Australia, with $250,000 in gold and silver bullion and specie. There is a report that part of the treasure was salvaged several years ago.

Catherine Adamson (17)

British steamer foundered August 4, 1857, in twenty fathoms, off North Head, offshore Sydney, New South Wales, Australia, with consignment of $100,000 in gold and silver specie.

Princeza (18)

British schooner foundered March 15, 1863, in shallow water, off the northern tip of South Moreton Island, offshore Redcliffe, Queensland, Australia, with consignment of United States gold and silver bullion and specie valued at $140,000.

Gothenberg (19)

British steamer foundered February 24, 1875, off Nares Rock, North Queensland, Australia, with $180,000 in gold specie in vessel's safe, plus an unknown amount of gold nuggets and dust which the miners who were drowned carried in their pouches.

General Grant (20)

American ship crashed into a cave on the western coast of Disappointment Island, New South Archipelago, March 18, 1866, with consignment of $15,000,000 in gold bullion and specie, in sixteen fathoms. An Australian syndicate has salvaged $3,500,000 to date.

Chatterton (21)

British steamer foundered in 1895, in forty-two fathoms, one and a half miles off Seal Rocks, offshore Sydney, New tralia, with $150,000 in gold and silver specie.

Carlisle Castle (22)

British steamer foundered July 12, 1899, in six fathoms, off Rockingham, on offshore rocks, near Perth, Western Australia, with $150,000 in gold and silver specie.

Elingamite (23)

British steamer foundered November 9, 1902, in twenty-five fathoms, on West King Island, one of the Three King's Islands, off the northern tip of New Zealand's North Island, with $140,000 in gold half-sovereigns and silver specie. In 1902, $11,000, and 1967, $1,200 in specie were recovered.

Cumberland (24)

British steamer foundered in 1917, in sixteen fathoms, four miles off Eden, Twofold Bay, New South Wales, Australia, with $340,000 in gold and silver specie and lead and copper ingots. To date some $90,000 has been recovered.

Niagara (25)

Canadian steamer was sunk by German mines on June 19, 1940, in seventy-three fathoms, twenty-eight miles off-shore, due north of Hauraki Gulf, New Zealand. The steamer carried a secret wartime consignment of the Bank of England, amounting to $12,500,000 in gold bullion. In 1941, $9,000,000 was salvaged.

Peary (26)

American destroyer sunk by Japanese bombs in 1942, in twenty-one fathoms, in outer Port Darwin harbor, Van Dieman Gulf, Northern Australia, with consignment of $2,500,000 in gold bullion, taken aboard at Manila, Phil. Ids., prior to Japanese seizure of the islands.

Other Treasure Craft (27)

Scores of Spanish (Manila) galleons, treasure-laden, wrecked during the seventeenth century, rest in the waters of Torres Strait, offshore the islands of Cape York, Thursday, Stephens, Prince of Wales, Booby, and on the Maubiege Reefs; and also along the Whitsunday Passage between the mainland of Australia and Whitsunday Island.

General Index

of Sunken Treasure Shipwrecks

by Name

The Lure

of "Buried" Treasure

BURIED TREASURE! The words are synonymous with mystery and glamor. The mere whisper of these words, like *Sunken Treasure*, works magic and conjures up visions of the fabulous riches that all mortals crave enough to risk anything for, even their most valuable possession—their lives. Down through the ages history has recorded evidence of craving for gold and silver which has brought great events and achievements which have, in turn, caused important historical changes and progress.

The Argonauts, the legendary Greek heroes, were the first people who, according to tradition, started the search for precious metals. According to legend, these peoples acquired renown by an adventurous journey into unknown seas in a ship called *Argo*, which sailed under the command of Jason, in their search for the Golden Fleece. This was the first gold rush on record.

The first mention of gold in the Bible appears in the second chapter of Genesis, 11th and 12th verses, wherein it makes mention of the Land of Havilah, *"where the gold groweth and is good."* This was before the time of Noah. Then, again, in Genesis XXIV, it is recorded that Abraham sent Rebecca jewelry in the form of earrings and bracelets, showing that gold and silver jewelry was part of the Jewish culture of the time. Later, too, the science of chemistry is depicted as owing its first development to the efforts of the ancient alchemists to discover a method of producing gold from other metals. Early hieroglyphics show that the ancient power of Egypt in its zenith had a revenue equal to thirty million dollars of our present-day currency per annum from its gold and silver mines.

The savages of Africa and South America had little use for the two metals other than for occasional ornamental purposes. Some fashioned their fish hooks from gold because they knew nothing of the use of iron. The American aborigines at first gave gold no more consideration than they did the pebbles in the creeks and rivers.

The early ancients used gold in quantity for ornamental uses only, but as civilization advanced and progressed, and pockets and clothing came into use, the indestructible, unchanging characteristics and mobility of the metal constantly increased its value as compared with other metals of lesser color. Eventually, gold displaced the use of iron as an exchange in Greece, where at one time, if a man desired to trade, he had to hitch up a yoke of oxen to a chariot, and take a ton of the metal to make the payment.

Then, as the years passed and the civilized peoples of Europe learned of the discovery of America in the fifteenth century, the fabulous legends of the wondrous glory and astonishing riches of the New World aroused and amazed the gold-and-silver-seeking minds of Europe, and expedition after expedition stampeded into the newly discovered regions.

Today, the mere thought of gold and silver fascinates

Fig. 1. A find of old Chinese artifacts and relics, unearthed from old Chinese section of early mining camp by buried treasure-seekers using electronic metal detectors. Shown are opium pipes and bowls, gambling markers, Chinese coins, etc.

Fig. 2. The famous Dogtown Nugget Memorial, at Megalia, Butte County, Calif. It commemorates the discovery of the 54-pound gold nugget in the canyon below. This same area still abounds in gold ore.

Fig. 3. Prospector's cabin more than 100 years old, showing gold pan, spade, and rocker (on right). It was located by a vacationing buried-treasure enthusiast.

Fig. 4. Wells, Fargo & Co.'s "reward poster," gun, skull, early American coins, early Colt pistol—all unearthed from a long-abandoned Old West mining camp.

Fig. 5. A small part of Frank L. Fish's private collection of relics and artifacts unearthed from abandoned mining camps of the Old West.

Fig. 6. A buried treasure find: Civil War saber, Colt cap-and-ball pistol of early vintage, and other artifacts unearthed in prospector's stone cabin of the Old West, located near a long-abandoned mining camp site.

Fig. 7. Copy of the long-sought and much prized map of the Lost Dutchman Mine. Known as the "Peralta Map," it located the mine just a few miles south of Phoenix, Arizona.

Fig. 8. One of the latest electronic metal detectors, used in locating old abandoned mines and bandit caches on land.

Fig. 9. Theron Fox and his daughter searching for buried treasure amid the remains of a long-abandoned site. They are using electronic metal-detecting equipment.

most men, and the golden gleam flashes back through dreams of the past; for an incalculable part of this long-buried—and often lost—wealth still rests, undisturbed and unearthed, waiting for adventurous modern-day explorers and prospectors to wrest it from its earthly resting-places, in thousands of places, in lost Spanish and other mines, and in old and abandoned mine sites. Thousands of enthusiasts are searching for it with the use of recent electronic metal detectors and other apparatus.

The hunt for "buried" treasure entices many, from the historian and archaeologist to the man who aspires to the wealth itself. The following pages of authenticated clues and potential sites is primarily addressed, as a guide, to the last-named, to those who may entertain ideas of tracking down gold or silver caches, some long-lost, others of more recent vintage.

The very considerable difficulties, however, should not be overlooked. At least three crucial questions face the would-be discoverer of lost or buried mines: Is the report of its existence genuine? Are the details of its supposed location reliable? If so, does the cache still await the seeker? The more precise the information, the less likely is it now to be of value; for obviously the site may have already been found, and the treasure itself unearthed. However, the possibilities are still exceptionally good, as earlier failures to find it may have been due to a lack of adequate and modern equipment; or the topography of the region may have changed to such an extent that vital landmarks no longer can be identified with certainty; or the directions may have been in code.

In the light of these possibilities, a representative selection of reputedly authentic sources of wealth is here presented. In assembling these listings, available evidence has been critically examined, and the records surveyed substantiate the potential accurateness of same. For the treasure-seeker, any one of these listings may yet prove to be the exact site of "treasure for the taking."

The Old West's

Lost Spanish Mines

IN THE FIFTEENTH CENTURY, when the civilized peoples of Europe learned of the discovery of gold and silver, the fabulous legends of the wondrous glory and astounding riches of the New World aroused and amazed the gold-and-silver-seeking minds of the Continent. And, in quick succession followed the conquests of Mexico and Peru for the yellow and white metals, under the leadership of the Spanish explorers Hernando Cortés and Francisco Pizarro. With Cortés' conquest of Mexico and Pizarro's conquest of Peru, the ravenous craving and passion for wealth and adventure were unbridled and became irrepressible.

New fields and new lands had long been sought by the Spanish, and attention finally was directed toward the mysterious regions of land of the great southwest. The new unexplored territory became the first conquest of the Spaniards in America, and many were the gold-and-silver-seeking expeditions to this new land sent out by these early Spanish explorers.

In 1534, the first Europeans to set foot on the soil of

153

this vast region were Alvar Nunez Cabeza de Vaca and his three companions. In fact, they were, indeed, the first white men to discover gold and silver. Actually, these explorers had approached the territory from the east in an endeavor to reach European civilization by way of a new western channel, in order to escape capture by the coastal Indian tribes which at the time inhabited the shores along what is today known as the Gulf of Mexico. They had previously been captured and held in captivity and slavery for several years when their party had been stranded on that coast by a disastrous shipwreck. Their discovery may be regarded therefore as one of mere accident or chance and not as conquest. In fact, it was Cabeza de Vaca who first recorded the discovery of turquoise by white men, when he and his party found it in abundance at the farthest point north of the Rio Grande valley, presumably located near the present site of Bernalillo, in what is now known as Sandoval county, New Mexico.

Five years later, in 1539, on hearing tales of Cabeza de Vaca's exploits and discoveries of this then-valuable turquoise-bearing land in this strange and mysterious new territory to the north, Friar Marcos de Niza immediately fitted out an expedition and traveled northward as far as what was then known as Cibola, now believed to be Zuni. This adventurous friar's expedition was more of a religious venture, with a view to the conversion of the aborigines in the region, than for wealth; but in his written reports, he speaks of seeing considerable blue turquoise stone and some gold and silver in the region.

Other explorers followed, and in 1540, the most notable of these early Spanish expeditions into the great southwest territory was made by the Spanish general Francisco Vasquez de Coronado and his army of followers, an expedition for conquest and the discovery of gold and silver. He had followed much the very same route overland as Friar Marcos de Niza, and he, too, finally arrived at Cibola (Zuni) on the ninth of July. Research substantiates unquestionably that Cibola was the old Zuni Indian Pueblo of today's western county of McKinley, close to the Arizona state line.

Shortly after Coronado's arrival at Cibola, he dispatched a captain in his army, one Alvarado, to go to the south and east and explore the regions. Although the exact route which they followed is somewhat obscure in the early historical records, it is known that the party drifted southeast, touching on the Rio Grande River near what was then called La Joya, which they followed upstream to a point at or near the present site of Bernalillo. There they again met Coronado and his forces and went into winter quarters until spring.

In May 1541, Coronado began his memorable march to the east and north in search of the famed legendary city of Quivira (not to be mistaken for Gran Quivira), which the Pueblo Indians had told of. In the middle of the summer he reached the ancient city and began searching for the gold and silver riches the Indians had reported existed there. However, the only metal of value which he saw at Quivira happened to be a small piece of copper which the chief of the Pueblo Indians wore around his neck, and which no doubt came from one of their ancient workings at the mines.

As Coronado had not found any gold or silver in quantity, he was disappointed and frustrated, and he again started southward with his forces toward the Rio Grande, where they camped and spent a second winter. From there, he ordered numerous short expeditions, under the command of various captains, sent out to the east, west, and northeast to explore more thoroughly the contiguous territory. On these various explorations some small amounts of turquoise and placer gold were discovered, though not to the extent of their expectations. So again not meeting with the success the explorers had hoped for in their searches, instead plagued with disaster, disappointment, and further frustration at their failure, General Coronado called his forces together and quit the region in 1542, thus ending the first great treasure hunt and conquest in the regions of the great southwest. However, from a humanitarian point of view, with respect to the treatment of the Pueblo Indians by his invaders, Coronado's expedition might be considered nothing more than organized highway robbery, rape of the aborigine women, and murder perpetrated on a peaceful and harmless populace.

Then, in 1580, just forty years after the expedition of Francisco Vasquez de Coronado, one Don Antonio de Espejo visited Cibola and several other sites in the region in search of the fabulous treasure mines which he had heard about. One of the strangest incidents which he encountered on his visit at Cibola was that of coming across a number of Christian Indians who had formerly accompanied Coronado into this strange land and who had remained instead of returning with their general to Mexico. They had apparently been converted by the Spanish priests on the expedition. They told Don Espejo of populous cities on the banks of a great lake, far to the northwest of Cibola, where gold and silver were so plentiful that the women of the tribes residing along the lake waters wore the metals in the form of bracelets and charms. It is believed that this great lake, as they called it, was later to be known as the Great Salt Lake, now in the state of Utah.

However, Don Espejo explored far into the territory, but did not find the lake the aborigines spoke about; on the contrary, he traveled far into the region which is today Arizona. The records show that he returned to the Rio Grande, from which he later made a journey to the northeast from some point on the river (the Colorado). And in this brief record it recounts: "Here they were informed by the aborigines of the rich mines of the precious metals, some of which they visited and took from them good glittering ore."

The next expedition by the Spaniards in their search for the precious metals in the southwest regions was started in June 1601, by one Oñate. Like his predecessors Coronado and Espejo, who, excited over the legends of the Indians, told of the fabulous riches lying to the far northeast, he started for Quivira. As Oñate's party proceeded on their journey of discovery, strange tales of great cities came to their ears from time to time, which stimulated and elated the hopes of the army of treasure-seekers. The aborigines told tales of this new region having utensils hammered out of the two metals, and of natives decorating their persons with ornaments of burnished gold and polished silver. However, after having chased this phantom of the imagination for some months without success, Oñate and his followers finally gave up the search and returned to San Juan in the first part of October, just before the winter set in, despairing and disappointed like those who had preceded him by some sixty-odd years.

In 1620, one Padre Geronimo de Zarate Salmeron, who headed an expedition to do missionary work among the aborigines, wrote about his travels and described the torrid climate in summer, the frigid cold in winter, and of finding some rich mines in the area. But, apparently disgusted and feeling considerable remorse over the extreme cruelties of his own countrymen toward the natives, the padre stated

that the Spaniard would enter the "doors of hell" in order
to satisfy his craving and gluttony for gold and silver wealth,
were it possible to obtain such metals from that new
territory.

Numerous other Spanish expeditions were sent out under various explorers during the one hundred years between
1580 and 1680, when the Pueblo Indians rose up against
the arrogant invaders. They could no longer endure the
hardships, forced slavery, and cruelties which the invading
Spaniards inflicted upon them, principally in the mines of
those who had found and operated them. The Spaniards
were forced to flee the territory as a result of their cruelties,
and when at the close of the seventeenth century they were
once more allowed to return, they were no longer permitted
to engage in mining activities—only in agricultural pursuits
which the Spaniards found not to their liking.

The Spaniards had ever been gold-and-silver-seekers
from the earliest times, and placer gold was the type of
mining which they knew most about; lode mines were not
so alluring to them. Although they did engage in some small
placer gold mining, no rich discoveries were ever brought
to notice by them with the exception of the old and new
placers; in fact, prior to 1680, the principal miners were
the Spanish Jesuits, and they were the ones whom the
Pueblo Indians mainly wreaked their vengeance upon in a
general massacre.

Both tradition and history have recorded that after the
uprising of the Pueblo Indians, all the known mines at the
time were filled in and completely covered up so that when
the Spaniards did return and were prohibited from mining,
the succeeding generations of aborigines were themselves
unable to locate them again. Also, during that temporary
exodus of both the Spaniards and Jesuits from the territory,

the records had been either destroyed by the Pueblos or were carried to Mexico—and some even back to Spain—by the fugitives in their desperate flight, resulting in the complete obliteration of all the early mines and mining records of the region.

What happened to these fabulous mines? The reports and legends of the wealth of some mystic *Eldorados* were to the conquering Spaniards ever a stimulus for further conquest of the aborigines. And even today these tales of "lost or hidden mines" have a considerable charm of romance and mystery woven about them, and it is never difficult to find new believers in such traditions and legends.

Too, it might be added that such tales have ever been the *ignes fatui* that have held many a later prospector and treasure-hunter spellbound and carried him far afield into the unknown stretches, ultimately resulting in giving to the world a Cripple Creek or a Klondike bonanza. The enchanted and ever-luring Adam's Diggings, the legendary Lost Peg-Leg-Lode, the mythical Log Cabin Mine, and many similar tales and legends of like "lost mines" actually exist in the imagination only; however, they have served well as a constant stimulus to the prospector who, in his search for wealth, with pick and pan, paves the way for civilization. Such fantasies, then, from an unprejudiced viewpoint, are to be regarded as real and necessary factors in the successful search for gold and silver lodes.

The exciting tales of long-lost Spanish mine sites—even those of buried riches from some bandit's hidden cache—are well known to the prospector and treasure-hunter, even to the general public. They usually have little substantiation, other than, perhaps, that of some Spaniard who returning to the region where his ancestors had presumably buried a fabulous treasure, located and perhaps worked the

mine, or of some bandit's hidden cache—often accompanied
with a hand-scrawled map of the particular locale. However,
perhaps, one of these days, as has happened so often in the
past, one will hear on the newscasts or read in the newspapers of a gold or silver mine or cache of this period of
early Spanish conquests having been rediscovered and unearthed in some region of these southwestern states.

Modern-day Jesuits endeavor to substantiate that there
was little gold or silver mined in these old Spanish mines,
but there must have been huge quantities produced, or else
why did these early explorers go to the effort of working
so many mines? However, both prospectors and lost-mine
seekers, so often while exploring these particular regions,
have unearthed high-grade gold and silver ores in huge
pieces from the dumps and tailings nearby. Many, therefore, are of the opinion that the returns from these now
"lost mines" and their diggings were the means of funding
the many missions prior to the expulsion of Jesuits and
other orders in 1767.

As numerous finds of paydirt ore have actually been
made in these areas from time to time, it stands to reason
that for the modern-day treasure-hunter, with his electronic
and geophysical equipment, these long-hidden caches are
still potential prospects which, though not big bonanzas,
today would be really worth their efforts in further
exploration.

These sites are but a few clues to the hundreds of
"lost mines" which the Spanish Jesuits left to posterity in
their search for the two precious metals, gold and silver,
wealth of the great southwest—long-buried riches which
have captivated the imaginations of treasure-seekers, stirred
the minds of men, and which continue to lead mankind as

ever into new fields on its constant quest for the gleaming yellow and white metals. *The signs are all there, and waiting!*

So here, for the benefit of those enthusiasts who seek clues to some of these long-hidden caches, are described the substantiated lost mines in this mysterious territory:

Treasure of Gran Quivira (1)

The early Pueblo Indian legends record that a vast treasure in gold and silver still rests buried beneath the remains of the old Spanish church of Gran Quivira in eastern Torrance County, New Mexico. The cache, it is claimed, was in the custody of the Jesuit priests at the time the community was destroyed by a volcanic eruption. Some of the ruins still exist, but the pueblo itself was likely contemporaneous with all of the other settlements of the time in the Rio Grande Valley, as the entire territory of the southwest was then known to the Spaniards, and passed into decadence from the very same causes that had obliterated almost every other aboriginal Indian pueblo.

The long-extinct volcanic crater, situated at the extreme north end of the great lava flow, known as the *mal pais*, is what archaeologists of the region have decided is the source which dealt destruction to the community. This huge crater is approximately forty miles to the south and a short distance east of Gran Quivira. Archaeological explorers have suggested that the Indian settlement itself may have been abandoned because seismic disturbances caused the water supply to sink in its natural basin.

The few ruins of Gran Quivira have been excavated to some extent at various periods by different persons who have been lured to the desolate site by traditions and legends in their search for buried riches. However, none has as yet brought forth any signs of either gold or silver of worth from any of the ruins.

Oldest Spanish Mines (2)

The oldest Spanish mines in America were those of the Spanish silver and turquoise operations, worked by the Jesuits from 1680 upward to 1800. These mines, worked for their silver ores, were called *Mina del Tierra*, and were near Cerrillos, New Mexico. Some years ago the diggings were briefly explored and found to consist of an incline shaft of 150 feet which connected with a somewhat vertical shaft of approximately 100 feet in depth. Here, extensive drifts of some 300 feet connected with various chambers or slopes, these being formed by stoping or mining out the richer ore bodies. However, the full extent of the workings has never been definitely determined, for the lower depths were then covered with water which would have to be pumped out to fully explore the mine further.

Yet, as late as 1870, the remains of an old Indian canoe were still in evidence below, the craft having been used for crossing the water in the mine, or as a carrier for conveying the waste and ore to the main shaft, from which it was then carried up to the surface on the backs of the aborigines in rawhide buckets or *tenates*. The deep shaft showed step-platforms or landings approximately every twelve or fourteen feet which were gained by climbing a notched pole (chicken ladder, as it was called), similar to what some of the Pueblo Indians still use at the present day. Numerous crude and curious relics, such as stone hammers and sledges, fragments of pottery, and other artifacts, have been taken from both the mine itself and the waste dump above. It is surmised that the Jesuits themselves had forced the aborigines to perform the work prior to 1680

Three Spanish Mines (3)

In Grant county, New Mexico, there are still the remains of several old Spanish gold mines. The *Santa Rita Mine*, long ago abandoned, is located on the south side of the Rio del Norte, just out of Whitewater. The *Santa Rosalia Mine*, in the Sierra de Oro, just west of the ancient Spanish mine known in its heyday as *Mina del Compromiso*, operated in 1833. The *Santo Nino Mine*, another old gold and silver diggings, lies in the Real San Francisco del Tuerte, in Santa Fe county, New Mexico.

Fabulous Spanish Cache (4)

A fabulous Spanish cache in Aztec treasure, which had been smuggled out of Old Mexico, estimated to be worth at least $12,000,000, is reported to be stored somewhere in an old mine tunnel known as the White Mountain Diggings. The actual site lies twenty miles northeast of Kanab, Utah, on the side of White Mountain, close to the petroglyphs in Johnson Canyon.

Jesuit Placer Site (5)

Close to what was known by the Indians as Spirit Springs (now Oak Springs), near Mesilla, New Mexico, in the Canada de la Madera, at the foot of a steep cliff, still rests a placer site worked by the Jesuits. A huge quantity of the unearthed gold and silver ore had been stored in the tiny Indian mission until the structure was suddenly demolished and washed into the canyon by a terrific torrent and deluge.

Stolen Relics of the Mission Santa Ysabel (6)

Somewhere just above the site of the early Butterfield Stage Station, in San Felipe, California, lie buried on a hillside the stolen relics of the old Mission Santa Ysabel. These filched treasures consist of the mission's first bells, the gold fixtures of the altar, and a large amount of gold and silver ore. According to the superstitious Indians, the site is a most sacred place, and they claim that a blue flame may still be seen hovering over the site.

Old Spanish Gold Mine (7)

Somewhere in the mountains just east of the San Juan Capistrano Mission are the caved-in tunnels of an old Spanish gold mine which the Jesuit missionaries worked until an earthquake obliterated the site and demolished the entrance.

Unidentified Jesuit Gold Mine (8)

An old Spanish Jesuit mine site lies just above the city of Redlands, near Yucaipa, California. The waste dump of the long-forgotten mine at one time was worked by the Jesuits using Indian slave labor in its operation. Even today, scattered hunks of high-grade gold ore are often unearthed from the tailings, though the mine shaft itself has never been actually located.

Virgin Guadalupe Mine (9)

In Santa Cruz county, Arizona, a few miles south of Tubac, and approximately four miles south of where the Tumacacori Mission once stood between the years 1508 and 1648, just north of the San Ramon River, in the Tumacacori Mountains, the early Spanish Jesuits worked a large silver mine called the *Virgin Guadalupe*. Today this vanished site is numbered among the "lost mines" of the region.

Lost San Pedro Mine (10)

This mine was once a flourishing silver mine, worked by the same group of Jesuit priests as that of the *Virgin Guadalupe*, and was located just four and a half miles west of the former Tumacacori Mission site.

Opata Silver Mine (11)

A short distance east of both the *Virgin Guadalupe* and the *Lost San Pedro* mine sites was this workings, resting in the western foothills of the San Cayetano Mountains for just a few miles.

Bella of Old Guevavi Mine (12)

This Jesuit mission silver workings was at a site at the extreme southwest end of the same rugged San Cayetano Mountains.

Escalante Mine (13)

This once-famous silver mine is also known as the *Mine With the Iron Door*. It is undiscovered to date, but it is known to lie in the Santa Catalina Mountains, close to Tucson, in Pima county, Arizona. It was one of the richest of all the Jesuit mining operations.

Lost Mine of Del Bac (14)

In the rugged mountains, seven miles southwest of the present-day Mission San Xavier del Bac, near Tucson, in Pima county, Arizona, on the San Xavier Indian Reservation, is the site of this early Jesuit silver mine.

Lost Dominican Silver Mine (15)

In 1777, the Dominican priests established and worked for many years a rich silver mine close to their Mission Santa Catrina Martyr, approximately fifty-eight miles south of La Rumorosa, in the Sierra de Juarez Mountains of Baja California, just across the border between the two countries. The site today is located halfway between Ojos Negro and Rancho Viego, some sixteen miles north of the tiny settlement of Rancho Viejo, on the old Trinidad Valley road.

Lost Mines of

the United States

HERE, for the first time, are listed clues to 150 lost mines the bandit caches. Silent and mysterious, they wait to be re-discovered.

The term "lost mines" is a misnomer. However, the derivative happens to be a part of speech to designate those early gold and silver mines and placers which were abandoned for a number of reasons. Often these mines were abandoned when the price of the metals dropped to such a low ebb that it became impossible or unprofitable to operate; some others were closed down when water seeped into their shafts and pumping the water out was too expensive; others were closed due to the long hauls from their usually isolated workings. And still others were abandoned by their operators due to death, murder—which was quite common during the heyday of the mining era—or other causes.

They are true lost mines, but in reality they are not lost at all.

However, hundreds of mines that, because of these and other causes, were not worked for such a long period were forgotten and their actual sites soon were covered by sand and earth, trees and scrub growth. The only records of their existence are to be found in obscure history books, dusty files of the early newspapers of the region, or long-forgotten government documents and records.

Even so, many of these so-called "lost mines" have been found by buried treasure-hunters and enthusiasts, and fortunes have and are continually being extracted from them with little, if any, publicity.

Searching for such sites takes thorough and tedious research through county libraries and early newspapers of the particular period when they existed; also, it is time-consuming to delve into the state historical files which specialize in and describe the region where the "lost mines" are located. Periodicals such as *Real West, Western Treasures, Treasure Hunters Guide, True Treasure, True West, Frontier Times, Old West,* and other like mediums, featuring true accounts of those once-fabulous diggings, often furnish exceptional leads.

After obtaining the probable location and other data, it goes without saying that the use of electronic metal-locating and geophysical apparatus may further bring the searcher within possible reach of his quest, with some persistence and a small amount of luck. One thing is certain: with the use of such devices, a turn of the spade, and some small amount of physical labor a good quantity of relics and artifacts, and often many thousands of dollars in gold and silver or other valuables, could turn up, even a fabulous fortune!

The search for these long-hidden mines can be most exciting and adventurous, and often quite lucrative. On the other hand, it can often become, with sudden unexpected problems or accidents, a most disastrous failure. For in pushing their search into usually unknown regions, the early prospectors who first discovered these illusive caches of gold and silver had to overcome vast unexplored distances and endure intense hardships and suffering. They also had to be constantly on the alert, since they were often hunted in the day and haunted at night by the savage hordes which infested these uncivilized areas.

Nevertheless, men are still continually seeking these once fabulous mines. The use of burros and mule teams has long ago vanished; jeeps and station wagons, fully equipped with electronic equipment, now replace them, making new trails into the out-of-the-way regions in their search for long hidden sites which still await the lucky finders.

Buried gold and silver is where one finds it, and so are the clues to "lost mines." However, if all the clues to "lost mines" were actually known, there would not be any lost mines.

For those who contemplate searching for these sites, the following true "lost mines" will furnish the modern-day prospector and treasure-hunter leads by state and county from which to make a start in their venture, probably to riches.

ARIZONA

Lost Blonde Mayo Mine

Apache county: on east side of Altar Valley, Black Princess Mt., in Cerro Colorado Mountains.

Lost Silver Monument Valley Mine

Apache county: near Mitchell Butte.

Lost Apache Girl Mine

Cochise county: on west side of old Fort Bowie, in Dos Cabeza Mountains.

Lost Skeleton Mine

Cochise county: in Skeleton Canyon, Peloncillo Mountains.

Lost John D. Lee Placer Mine

Coconino county: in canyon above Vulture's Throne, Grand Canyon.

Lost Tonto Apache Mine

Coconino county: near Sedona.

Lost Coconino Mine

Coconino county: at extreme southwest corner of county, twenty miles southwest of Flagstaff.

Lost Deadman Mine

Coconino county: southwest of Cameron.

Lost Morgan Mine

Coconino county: south of Flagstaff.

Lost Sander's Mine

Gila county: on north slope, ten miles from head of Coon Creek, in Sierra Anchas Mountains.

Lost Apache Mine

Gila county: on north slope of Mt. Ord, Tonto Basin.

Lost Black Burro Mine

Greenlee county: northeast of Clifton, between junction of San Francisco and Blue rivers.

Lost Lord Duppa Mine

Maricopa county: near Wickenburg.

Lost Pick Mine

Maricopa county: in Bronco Canyon, twenty-five miles northwest of Fort McDowell.

Lost Squaw Hollow Mine

Maricopa county: forty miles northeast of Phoenix, in Squaw Hollow.

Lost Nugget Mine

Mohave county: near Wikieup.

Lost Cerro Colorado Mine

Pima county: on south slope, northeast of Arivaca, in Cerro Chiquita Mountains.

Lost Cienega Bender's Mine

Pima county: thirty miles southeast of Tucson, near old stage station of Cienega, Pantano.

Lost Fortuna Mine

Pima county: east of Tucson.

Lost Carreta Canyon Mine

Pima county: in foothills, near Arivaca, Tascosa Mountains.

Lost Escalante Mine

Pima county: on south bank of Canada del Oro river, northeast of Tucson, in Catalina Mountains.

Lost Esmeralda Mine

Pima county: east nf Tucson.

Lost Orphan Mine

Pima county: near Tule Tank, in Cabeza Prieta Mountains.

Lost Papago Gold Mine

Pima county: near Ajo.

Lost Sopon Gold Mine

Pima county: between Tucson and Arivaca.

Lost Waggoner's Mine

Pima county: on south slope of La Barge Canyon, between Weaver's and Miner's Needle, in Superstition Mountains.

Lost Coyotero Mine

Pinal county: at north end of Toto Basin, Mogollon Rim.

Lost Soldier's Mine

San Carlos county: between east Boulder and Needle Canyons.

Lost Doc Thorne's Mine

Santa Cruz county: in White Mountains.

Lost Don Miguel Peralta Mine

Santa Cruz county: in La Barge Creek, La Barge Canyon, Superstition Mountains.

Lost La Purisima Concepcion Mine

Santa Cruz county: fifteen miles southwest of Tumacacori Mission's west end, near Cerro Ruido Mt., El Pajarito Mountains.

Lost Major Peoples' Mine

Santa Cruz county: in hills extending to Hassayampa river, southeast of Congress Junction.

Lost Geronimo's Gold Mine

Yavapai county: close to Verde River, between Jerome and Parkinsville, in Sycamore Canyon.

Lost Organ Grindor Mine

Yavapai county: on Cottonwood Creek, west of Prescott, in Peoples Canyon.

Lost Apache Gold Mine

Yavapai county: between Jerome and Parkinsville, in Sycamore Canyon.

Lost Nigger Ben's Mine

Yavapai county: at foot of Antelope Peak, east of Congress Junction.

Lost Squaw Hollow Mine

Yavapai county: near Camp Creek.

Lost Bicuner Gold Mine

Yuma county: near Squaw Creek, in Laguna Mountains.

Lost Belle McKeever Mine

Yuma county: west end, in Granite Mountains.

Lost Trigos Silver Mine

Yuma county: at foot of Clip Mt., in Trigos Mountains.

Lost Castle Dome Mine

Yuma county: on Colorado River, between Old King of Arizona Mine and Ehrenberg.

Lost John Nummel's Mine

Yuma county: on Colorado River, between Norton's Landing and Yuma Wash.

Lost Squaw Mine

Yuma county: between Yuma and Phoenix.

Lost Treasure of Rancho De La Yumas

Yuma county: on Colorado River's east bank, forty miles north of Yuma.

Lost Six-Shooter Mine

Yuma county: on Bill Williams River, between Quartzite and the old mining camp of Planet, fifteen miles northeast of Parker.

Lost Sopori Mine

Yuma county: at foot of Black Princess Peak, north end, in Cerro Colorado Mountains.

Lost Lead Mine

Yuma county: at extreme north end of Harquahala Mountains.

ARKANSAS

Lost Diamond Mine

Pike county: east of Murfreesboro.

Lost William Flynn's Diggings

Washington county: east of Murfreesboro.

CANADA

Lost Creek Gold Mine

British Columbia: three miles southeast of Mt. Manquam, two and a half miles west of Pitt River, near southern border of Garibaldi National Park.

CALIFORNIA

Lost Golden Caverns

Calaveras county: at lower end of French Gulch, near Columbia.

Lost Yankee Hill Mine

Calaveras county: buried in tubs in cave, near Columbia.

Lost Cabin Mine

Del Norte county: south of Crescent City, near mouth of Klamath River.

Lost Black Butte Mine

Imperial county: on Black Butte slope east of Ogilby, in Cargo Mountains.

Lost Hank Brandt's Mine

Imperial county: eighteen miles northwest of El Centro, in Superstition Mountains.

Lost Bullring Mine

Imperial county: in Mule Springs Canyon, Black Hills.

Lost Alec Ramy's Mine

Inyo county: on southern portion base of Dry Mt., in Last Chance Mountains.

Lost Alvord Mine

Inyo county: in Butte Valley, Panamint Mountains.

Lost Burro Mine

Inyo county: in Lost Burro Gap, Death Valley.

Lost Gunsight Mine

Inyo county: at lower entrance of Butte Valley, in Panamint Mountains.

Lost Old Clothes Mine

Inyo county: at extreme north tip of Avawatz Mountains.

Lost Panamint City Mine

Inyo county: on west side of Panamint Mountains.

Lost Skiddo Mine

Inyo county: on west side Emigrant Pass.

Lost Carry-Cart Mine

Kern county: in Mountain Springs Canyon, out of Ridge-crest, under one of seven lava flows in Argus Mountains.

Lost Frazier Mountain Mine

Kern county: somewhere in a tunnel above Chucapate Park.

Lost Chance Mine

Kern county: two to six miles north of White River.

Lost Goler Diggings

Kern county: in Goler Canyon, thirty-two miles north of Mojave.

Lost Mexican Mine

Kings county: sixty miles northeast of Visalia.

Lost Captain Dick Mine

Lassen county: northwest of Eagleville, between Pine Valley and Owl Creek, in Warner Mountains.

Lost Agua Fria Mine

Mariposa county: on outskirts of Agua Fria.

Cave of Escondido Mine

Mariposa county: in cave near Bagby, on Merced River.

Lost Frenchman's Flat Gold Mine

Mariposa county: below ghost town on small creek, near French Mills.

Lost Sierra Rica Mine

Mariposa county: three to five miles from Midpines.

Lost Whispering Pines Gold Mine

Mariposa county: near Midpines.

Lost Bodie Mine

Mono county: near Bridgeport.

Lost Dogtown Mine

Mono county: near Bridgeport.

Lost Iowa Hill Mine

Placer county: at head of East Fork of American River.

Lost Black Magic Mine

San Bernardino county: near Owl Hot Springs.

Lost Chuckawalla Wilson Mine

San Bernardino county: near Mitchell State Park, in Providence Mountains.

Lost Arch Diggings

San Bernardino county: at north end of Turtle Mountains, twenty-five miles north of Rice.

Lost Lee Mine

San Bernardino county: north of Old Woman's Well, in San Bernardino Mountains.

Lost New Deal Mine

San Bernardino county: near Owl Hot Springs.

Lost Sheephole Mountain Mine

San Bernardino county: near Amboy, northwest end Sheep Hole Mountains.

Lost Van Duzen Canyon Mine

San Bernardino county: between Gold Mountain and Bertha Peak, in Holcomb Valley.

Lost Nigger Hill Mine

San Joaquin county: near Mokelumne Hill, on north bank of San Antonio Creek.

Lost Humbug Creek Mine

Shasta county: near Redding, on western side of Humbug Mountain.

Lost Waterfall Mine

Shasta county: near Linwood, on Bear Creek, in Bear Canyon.

Lost Frenchman Mine

Siskiyou county: near Happy Camp, on Indian River.

Lost Big Oak Flat Mine

Toulumne county: near Big Oak Flat, on north side of Yosemite Road.

Lost Frenchman Mine

Yuba county: near Nevada City, on Grizzly Hill, in Frenchman's Canyon.

COLORADO

Lost Brush Creek Mine

Eagle county: [1]

1. The following description of the mine site was given by its discoverer to a physician who attended him just before his death: "Take the Denver & Rio Grande Railroad to Tennessee Pass; from there take the wagon road and trail along Eagle river to mouth of Brusk Creek; follow up the creek five miles to the forks, then take along the east branch five miles until coming to a shift of rocks, coming almost at the water's edge; from there a dry gulch runs north. Follow the gulch until coming to four large trees standing close together, with the bark all taken off, about two feet around them; then turn due east and directly up the hill will appear dug in the ground; keep directly on until coming to another one and so on until reaching the third one; this line is also marked by blazed trees on both sides; here turn due north and about 200 feet from the last blazed tree will appear three tall trees standing in a triangle, which trees have their tops broken off some thirty feet above ground level; this is about 300 feet from timberline, and the vein runs north and south from here; on top of the hill one can view the Mountain of the Holy Cross and west, the Taylor range."

Lost Spanish Peaks Mine

Huerfano county: in canyon at foot of Spanish Peaks Mountains.

Lost Reynolds Bandit Cache
Park county: [2]

GEORGIA

Lost Old Billy Chambles Mine

Gwinnett county: Off Highway 23, three miles north of Swanee Creek, off Beaver Ruin Creek.

IDAHO

Lost Sly Meadows Gold

Benewah county: at Sly Meadows on Bond Creek's west fork of St. Joe River.

Lost Swim Gold Mine

Chalis county: on Moley Creek above Robinson's Bar, south of Bonanza on the Salmon River.

---

2. Buried somewhere up Handcart Gulch, in Hall Valley, is the Reynolds bandit cache, estimated at more than $100,000 in gold, which had been accumulated by the notorious hijackers who terrorized the South Park mining camp, holding up stagecoaches and lone riders.

Lost Rock Bandit Cache

Clark county: [3]

Lost Indian Post Office Mine

Clearwater county: near Indian Post Office cairn, close to Cayuse Junction.

Lost Sunken Ore of Lake Coeur

Coeur d'Alene county: [4]

Lost Bill Rhodes Mine

Idaho county: near Grave Peak, in Lolo National Forest.

Lost Isaac Gold Mine

Idaho county: on Coolwater Ridge near Indian Springs, between Selway and Locksa rivers, on Coolwater Mountain.

Lost Rusted Wheelbarrow Mine

Latah county: in Thatuna Hills, of the Moscow Mountains.

Lost Breen Gold Diggings

Kootenai county: in rock tunnel, near Hayden Lake.

3. Cache of the infamous Plummer Gang's stagecoach robbery, consisting of $75,000 in gold bullion, buried a short distance above the town of Spencer, in Beaver Canyon.
4. One hundred and forty tons of gold ore from mines, sunk with steamer's barge *Kootenai*, November 12, 1889, in seventy-five feet of water, 300 feet offshore McDonald's Point, in Lake Coeur d'Alene.

Lost Cleveland Gold Mine

Lemhi county: near Wallace Creek, twelve miles above Salmon and eight miles from Salmon.

MAINE

Lost Lead Mountain Gold Mine

Hancock county: between Lead Mt., Ponds and Lead Mountain.

Lost Pirate Cache

Hancock county: on Swan Island, in Kennebec River.

Lost Pirate Buried Cache

Sagadahoc county: off Harpswell Neck, on Haskell Island.

Lost Pond Island Cache

Sagadahoc county: in Casco Bay, on Pond Island. Buried by Boston pirate Edward Low, taken from Spanish galleon commanded by Don Pedro del Monclova.

MEXICO

Lost Kelly Mine

Coahuila: between Maravillas Springs and Reagan Canyon, in Maravillas Canyon.

MISSISSIPPI

Lafitte's Gold Cache

Choctaw county: on four-acre patch of former cotton land, near old Natchez Trace, close to railhead of Mathestown.

NEVADA

Lost Pogue Mine

White Pine county: north of Pogue Station, in Pankake Mountains.

NEW MEXICO

Lost Skeleton Canyon Mine

Hidalgo county: in Skeleton Canyon, near Rodeo.

Lost Journada De La Muerto Mine

Sierra county: on eastern slope of Mt. Soledad, in Andreas Mountains.

Lost Acoma Silver Mine

Valencia county: off Highway 66, near Acoma and Laguna pueblos, in vicinity of McCartys.

NEW YORK

Lost Blenheim Silver Mine

Schoharie county: on northern side of Mt. Utsayantha.

NORTH CAROLINA

Lost Indian Silver Mine

Cherokee county: between Marble and Andrews.

OKLAHOMA

Lost Frenchmen's Cache

Cimarron county: on Sugarloaf Peak, northwest of Boise City. (Six carts of gold bullion valued at $2,000,000.)

Lost Bat Cave Platinum Mine

Creek county: in cave northwest of Meers, in Slick Hills.

Lost Spanish Mines

Jackson county: in Devil Canyon, north of Altus.

Lost Gold Bell Mine

Kiowa county: north of Snyder, near ghost town of Wildman.

Lost Chief Blackface Cache

Latimer county: in cave near Robbers Cave, north of Wilburton. (100 mule loads of gold ore.)

Lost Devil's Half Acre Mine

Okfuskee county: eight miles south of Okemah.

Lost Spanish Gold Mine

Sequoyah county: east of Spiro, on Buzzard Hill.

Lost Spanish Cache

Sequoyah county: bandit cache in cave, north of Sallisaw at foot of Brushy Mt.

OREGON

Lost Four Dutchman Gold Mine

Crook county: in canyon, just outside Prineville, in Ochoco Mountains.

Lost Soldier Mine

Douglas county: eleven miles west of Glendale, in mountain depression, on West Fork Cow Creek.

Lost San Pedro Mine

Lane county: on Big Inlet Creek, southeast slope of Diamond Peak.

Lost Sheepherder Mine

Malheur county: in desert between Freezeout Mt. and Owyhee River, just out of Coyote Wells.

Lost Malheur Mine

Malheur county: on Malheur Indian Reservation, thirteen miles from Agency.

Lost Tillamook Mine

Tillamook county: in Tillamook Burn, west of Gales Creek.

Lost Bear Creek Mine

Wallowa county: in Wallowa Mountains.

TENNESSEE

Lost Delosie Silver Mine

Sevier county: near North Carolina state border line.

TEXAS

Lost Nigger Bill Mine

Brewster county: at mouth of Reagan Canyon, in Big Bend National Park.

Lost Silver Ledge Mine

Dickens county: in Croton Brakes Canyon.

Lost Jim Bowie Mine

Menard county: near Menard, on San Saba River.

Lost San Saba Gold Mine

Menard county: near Menard, on San Saba river, just above old military fort's remains.

Lost Spanish Fort Mine

Montague county: abandoned by French settlement, near Spanish Fort, one mile south of Red River, in lake now drained two miles southeast of the old fort.

UTAH

Lost Spanish Cache

Kanab county: twenty miles northeast of Kanab, in petroglyph region of Johnson Canyon.[5]

Lost Spanish Mine

Millard county: in North Canyon, near Margum Pass.

5. Gold nuggets, gold dust, silver ornaments and shields, gold plates and cuirasses, pendants and bracelets studded with emeralds, rubies, and pearls, smuggled out of Mexico and hidden somewhere in Johnson Canyon.

Loot Margum Pass Mine

Millard county: at base of Swasey Peak, in canyon.

VERMONT

Lost Birch Hill Silver Mine

Rutland county: near Pittsford.

VIRGINIA

Lost Old Slave Cache

Fauquier county: off Highway 29, on Snow Hill Farm land, near Baltimore, buried near remains of Old Slave Barn.

WASHINGTON

Lost Shovel Creek Mine

Asotin county: near Craig, on Snake River.

Lost Ostrander Creek Mine

Cowlitz county: just outside Ostrander.

Lost Swauk Creek Mine

Kittitas county: off Highway 10 east, four miles out of Liberty, close to Elum, on Swauk Creek.

Lost Robber's Roost Cache

Pacific county: bandit cache, buried near Fort Columbia's Military Reservation, near Fruitland.[6]

Lost Spanish Gold Mine

Yakima county: near head of Lewis River, on northern slope of Mt. Adams.

WYOMING

Lost Docony Gold Mine

Albany county: in Laramie Hills.

Lost Martinez Mine

Albany county: in Laramie Hills.

Lost Spanish Gold Diggings

Platte county: just northeast of Glendo.

6. Buried bandit cache of gold nuggets, estimated to exceed $200,000, by Captain James Scarborough.

Old and

Abandoned Mines

THE UNITED STATES TREASURY DEPARTMENT is in need of both gold and silver, and today is encouraging modern-day prospectors "to mine more of the two metals." Here then, are more than 450 authenticated sites waiting for recoveries.

Modern-day prospecting for gold and silver in old and abandoned mine sites still pays the seeker. However, it being a new field of endeavor quite different from that which those hardy miners and prospectors followed in the past, today's search for these long-buried claims is being achieved through the use of electronic metal-detecting apparatus. It consists of the pickings of abandoned mining camps and diggings, both placer and lode, forgotten claims, bandit caches, and in some instances the sites of ghost towns long years ago disintegrated, scattered about in the out-of-the-way places of the Old West.

How the early prospectors and explorers, who first discovered most of these mining sites, ever managed to find their way through the intricacies of forbidding rugged mountains intersected by valleys, deep and treacherous gorges,

narrow canyons, and torrid desert regions to where the
pockets of gold and silver ore lay, continues to excite and
mystify the imagination.

Even when these adventurers reached a vein or pocket
of ore, one still wonders just how they maintained the supply lines for food, clothing, and equipment to both exist
and carry out their digging of the ores. Their courage and
endurance challenges even the contemplation of such feats.
Just, for example, drive over a main highway and note the
long-abandoned mine-shaft-houses perched, in many instances, atop inaccessible crags, standing alone on a
desert's sandy canyon. Or force your car over an old abandoned roadway which once led to the mine site, up steep
grades that even today would be considered intolerable,
or finally reach a rutted road only to have it suddenly dis-
appear, forcing you to leave your car and proceed on foot.

During the early sixties gold was practically the only
metal sought; in the seventies gold was still sought but silver
was found; and during the years of the eighties and nineties
the latter was sought to a greater degree and would have
continued to be sought had not the metal been demonetized
in 1893. The early sixties were rich for the placers, when
prospectors and miners followed the streams in search of
color and, when they discovered it, staked off claims and
began to pan the river and creek beds and banks. Others
soon left the streams to scramble up the mountainsides seeking "float" or exposed ore.

Then lode mining followed, the miners sinking their
shafts deep into the earth and tunneling into the mountainsides in search of the veins. The deeper the mines were
sunk and developed, the more varied and immovable the
ore deposits became, and other methods of extraction became necessary, Soon smelters and chlorination, lixivation,

and reduction plants were erected, each equipped to cope by chemical processes with the complex ore bodies. Later, improved methods of milling were installed in many of the larger mining camps to recover valuable minerals both by reworking the older mine dumps and by producing concentrates of the low-grade ores. Thus many a mining camp was deserted long before its paying ores were completely exhausted, simply because limited methods of milling failed to extract all the values obtainable. Today, in most of these mine sites, such tailings still remain for the taking by both prospector and treasure-seekers.

Also, many of these old mining sites cannot always be classified according to the particular metal, gold or silver, that was originally mined during their heyday, for later they grew up around a single mine or group of mines, all producing one metal, perhaps gold. Usually these mines flourished until, in time, the one ore played out, vanished; then the miners and prospectors departed and the mine itself became dormant or deserted. Later on other prospectors and miners came and discovered traces of another metal, perhaps silver, and soon another boom was on until the silver crash in 1893. Again the mines slept until some new seeker found tailings, and on and on such procedures continued. Today, again the search is on for the ores still remaining; this time by the modern-day prospector who seeks a fortune with smaller discoveries.

These smaller fortunes still rest within reach of anyone with adventure in his heart, and a fine mixture of courage and enthusiastic desire for riches. For those whom the words "buried treasure" cause their pulse to quicken, and perhaps force them to take a new interest in life with a new and thrilling hobby, or even a desire for profit, those who heretofore never have considered seeking such discoveries will find this new field of recreation and avocation a new thrill.

True, locating such long-buried caches may take a bit of doing, but it *can* be done. There are many individuals today, living in ease and comfort, who make a regular business from this sort of bizarre exploration; for untold numbers of both men and women from all walks of life are being lured into this exploring field for both recreation, adventure, and profit.

There is nothing magic about searching for buried treasure in old mining camps and ghost towns, in the desert, the mountains, and along the river and creek beds, where much of these riches still exist. It is a matter of knowing thoroughly, exactly *where* to search, *what* to seach for, and how to prepare for the search venture; a matter of acclimatizing to the rigors of the particular region in which such explorations are to be carried out. The game of "hunt the treasure" requires a rather specialized knowledge, training, talent, and enthusiasm. It is really quite simple, requiring electronic metal-detecting apparatus, easily acquired practice in the equipment's use—*and most of all the knowledge of where to search!*

The matter of *where* to search, which is a necessity, is usually the most difficult to come by, although it is a requirement. A general knowledge of *where* these long-abandoned sites were during their heyday of production furnishes the information to piece together a few nebulous facts about the mine site itself before undertaking exploratory operations.

The United States Treasury Department is in need of both gold and silver today, and is encouraging both prospectors and mining enthusiasts to "*mine more of the two metals.*" Contrary to popular belief, the United States has plenty of unmined gold and silver. Acording to a recent engineering survey in 1967 by the Bureau of Mines, there are more than 400,000,000 ounces of unmined gold in some 1,300 active mines and inactive sites of abandoned former mines in the western states waiting for unearthing of the precious metal. For this metal (gold) the Treasury Department pays thirty-five dollars per ounce; however, the going price is seventy dollars per ounce on the black market— almost all countries outside of the United States.

For those contemplating such an exploratory search for old and abandoned mine sites from which they might unearth treasure from the mines themselves or from the tailings, the following listings of authenticated old mines in these western states, and other potential sites, is furnished in the following pages to aid in pinpointing the exact locations *where* these fabulous long-hidden caches may still be found.

Good gold and silver hunting!

ARIZONA

Cochise County:

Dos Cabezos Mine
18 miles SE Wilcox
Cabezos Mts.

Gleeson Mine
20 miles E Tuscon.

Golden Rule Mine
E side Dragon Pass.

Hill-top Mine
NW Portal,
Chiricahua Mts.

Lavender Mine
SE Bisbee.

Middlemarch Mine
5 miles SW Pearce.

Paradise Mine
8 miles NW Portal,
Chiricahua Mts.

Pearce Mine
Near Sulphur Springs.

Prospect Mine
E side San Pedro Valley,
On Turkey Creek.

Pyramid Mine
75 miles SE Tombstone.

Reef Mine
8 miles W Hereford,
Huachuca Mts.

Roberts Mine
20 miles SE Wilcox.

Gila County:

Arizona Commercial Mine
5 miles N Globe.

Black Warrior Mine
7 miles NW Globe.

Boston Mine
5 miles N Globe,
On Copper Hill.

Crowley Mine
In Apache Mts.

Iron Cap Mine
5 miles N Globe,
On Copper Hill.

Julius Mine
9 miles E Globe,
Quartzite Mts.

Black Morris Mine
20 miles N Globe.

McMillen Mine
22 miles NE Globe.

Nugget Mine
3 miles N Richmond
Basin.

Oxbow Mine
Between Payson and
Roosevelt.

Pioneer Mine
W side Silver Creek,
Pinal Mt.

Silver Nugget Mine
14 miles N Globe.

Superior Mine
4 miles N Globe,
On Copper Hill.

Greenlee County:

Ash Creek Mines
Near Hardy,
On Ash Creek.

Metcalf Mine
8 miles E Metcalf,
On Chase Creek.

Oro Mine
4 miles E Clifton,
On San Francisco River.

Maricopa County:

Easter Mine
Near Easter
(just outside).

Judson Mine
Near Edith,
(outside Phoenix).

Mohave County:

American Flag Mine
W side Hualpai Mts.

Climax Mine
6 miles S Hualpai
Landing,
Virginia Canyon, Lake
Mead.

Cyclopic Mine
NW Kingman.

Diamond Joe Mine
On Big Sandy River.

German Mine
4 miles SE Oatman.

Golconda Mine
In Cerbat Mts.

Gold Basin Mine
40 miles N Kingman,
In Hualpai Wash.

Gold Road Mine
30 miles SW Kingman.

Greenwood Mine
Near Greenwood City
(just outside).

Hardyville Mine
Near Bullhead City.

Horn Silver Mine
7 miles NE Boulder Inn
Station.

King Tut Mine
14 miles S Pierce Ferry
Landing,
Lake Mead.

McCracken Mine
SW Wickieup.

Mineral Park Mine
Near Chloride.

Mohave Mine
Needles, Calif, (just outside).

Oatman Mine
Near Bullhead City.

Oro Plata Mine
4 miles S Mineral Park.

Pope Mine
9 miles NE Boulder Inn
Station.

Prosperity Mine
6 miles S Mineral Park.

Secret Mine
16 miles E Colorado
River,
In Black Mts.

Signal Mine
Needles, Calif. (just outside).

Stockton Hill Mine
8 miles SE Mineral Park,
NE slope Cerbat Mts.

White Hills Mine
Needless, Calif. (just outside).

Pima County:

Bates Well Mine
14 miles S Ajo.

Cerro Colorado Mine
42 miles S Tuscon.

Dowling Mine
Ajo Valley,
S end Sonoita Mts.

Esperanza Mine
W Sahiarita.

Gunsight Mine
On Papago Indian Reser-
vation,
Near W boundary.

Heintzeman Mine
42 miles S Tucson.

Horseshoe Mine
S end Quyotoa Mts.

Mammoth Mine
30 miles W Marana.

Mineral Hill Mine
On Tucson-Nogales Road.

Old Boot Mine
28 miles W Marana.

Olive Mine
W Santa Cruz.

Rosemont Mines
Furnace Gulch,
In Santa Rita Mts.

San Xavier Mine
On Santa Cruz River.

Silver Bell Mine
35 miles W Marana.

Vekol Mine
W side Cimarron Mts.

Pinal County:

American Flag Mine
Near Oracle,
Catalina Mts.

Reynert Mine
10 miles SW Superior.

Schultz Mine
10 miles NE Oracle.

Silver King Mine
Near Pinal City.

Santa Cruz County:

Austerlitz Mine
On Arivaca-Peña Lake.

Duquesne Mine
16 miles NE Nogales,
E side Patagonia Mts.

French Mine
20 miles NE Nogales.

Luttrell Mine
Near Lochiel.

Oro Blanco Mine
9 miles SE Arivaca.

Salero Mine
Foot of Salero Peak,
Santa Rita Mts.

Washington Mine
Near Washington,
E side Patagonia Mts.

Yavapai County:

Bluebell Mine
6 miles W Mayer

Chaparral Mine
W Humboldt.

Congress Mine
5 miles N Congress Jct.

Crown King Mine
In Bradshaw Mts.
Federal Mine
11 miles Cornville.

Goodwin Mine
Near Prescott,
On Turkey Creek.

Iron King Mine
Near Walker (just outside).

Jersey Lily Mine
24 miles S Prescott.

Placeritas Mine
8 miles E Peoples' Valley,
NE end Weaver Mts.

Richinber Mine
5 miles E. Bumblebee
Station,
On Aqua Fria River.

Senator Mine
Near head of Hassayampa
River.

Tip Top Mine
Near Kirbyville,
On Castle Creek.

Yuma County:

Castle Dome Mine
34 miles N Yuma,
In Castle Dome Mts.

Fortuna Mine
24 miles SE Yuma,
N side Sheep Mt.

Kofa Mine
30 miles S Quartzsite.

La Paz Mine
6 miles N Ehrenberg.

CALIFORNIA

Butte County:

Bader Mine
1½ miles E Magalia.

Black Diamond Mine
N De Sabla,
Off Ponderosa Way Road.

Blue Hog Mine
5 miles N Magalia.

Bumble Bee Mine
Between Oroville and
Oregon City.

Emma Mine
N Nimshew Cemetery.

Era Mine
Near Dry Creek.

Gaumer Mine.
On Dry Creek.

Genie Mine
½ to 1½ miles N Magalia.

Golden Nugget Mine
W slope West Branch
Feather River.

Indian Springs Mine
Near De Sabla.

Lucky John Mine
2 miles N Paradise.

Lucratia Mine
N Sawmill Peak.

Madre de Oro Mine
Near Paradise, S Ponderosa Way Road.

Magalia Mine
Near Magalia Camp.

Mineral Slide Mine
3 miles SE Magalia.

Old Utah Mine
N Empire Creek.

Oro Fino Mine
On Butte Creek, near De Sabla.

Princess-Cory Mine
2½ miles NE Magalia.

Road.
Royal Drift Mine
Near forks of Butte Creek, Ponderosa Way

Steifer Mine
Near Magalia Camp.

Inyo County:

Albertoli Mine
E Bishop, in Black Canyon.

Amargosa Mine
2 miles Salt Spring.

American Mine
Foot Ibex Peak, Ibex Hills.

Argus Sterling Mine
12 miles S Darwin.

Arro Gordo Mine
9 miles NE Keeler.

Ashford Mine
6 miles NE Ashford Jct., Death Valley.

Big Four Mine
7 miles N Panamint Springs.

Big Silver Mine
In Daisy Canyon.

Bunker Hill Mine
12 miles N Willow Creek.

Burgess Mine
Outside Lone Pine.

Cerro Gordo Mine
6 miles E Keeler.

Columbia Mine
3 miles N Tecopa Pass.

Crystal Spring Mine
2 miles N Crystal Spring.

Darwin Mine
2 miles NE Darwin.

Defense Mine
6 miles W Ash Hill Road,
Panamint Springs.

Desert Hound Mine
6 miles NE Ashford Jct.,
Death Valley.

Eclipse Mine
5 miles off Hwy No. 127,
Ibex Hills.

El Conejo Mine
6 miles W Howard Ranch,
Etcheron Valley.

Eureka Gold Mine
In Cowhorn Valley,
Eureka Valley.

Gladstone Mine
5 miles off Hwy No. 127,
Ibex Hills.

Golden Lady Mine
4 miles W Ash Hill Road,
Panamint Springs.

Grandview Mine
10 miles E Bishop.

Grant Mine
4 miles NW Ibex Pass.

Gray Eagle Mine
Near Bishop,
In Black Canyon.

Ibex Mine
5 miles Ibex Springs.

Keane Wonder Gold Mine
4 miles SW Cloride City.

Keeler Mine
Ulida Flat,
Death Valley.

Lee Mines
6 miles N Hwy No. 190,
Santa Rosa Hills.

Lemoigne Mine
Lemoigne Canyon,
Cottonwood Mts.

Lone Indian Mine
On Willow Creek,
Cowhorn Valley.

Lotus Mine
3 miles W Sourdough
Springs.

Mammoth Mine
6 miles NW Ibex Pass.

Mariposa Mine
2 miles S Mariposa Spring,
near Darwin.

Mexican Mine
10 miles E Bishop, on
South Fork.

Minnietta Mine
3 miles W Ash Hill Road,
Panamint Springs.

Modoc Mine
3½ miles Ash Hill Road,
Panamint Springs.

Mohawk Mine
2 miles S Homewood
Creek.

Mollie Gibson Mine
3 miles N Payson West-
gard Pass,
On Mollie Gibson Creek.

Montezuma Mine
4 miles NE Tenemaha
Reservoir.

Morningstar Mine
9 miles NE Keeler.

Noonday Mine
3 miles N Tecopa Pass.

Orondo Mine
2 miles N Homewood
Creek.

Onyx Gold Mine
10 miles W Ballarat, in
Sheperd Canyon.

Paddy Pride Mine
5 miles off Hwy No. 127,
in Ibex Hills.

Poleta Mine
4 miles E Bishop.

Porter Mine
9 miles E Ballarat.

Radcliff Mine
4 miles SE Ballarat.

Rusty Pick Mine
In Ibex Hills.

Ruth Mine
2 miles S Homewood
Creek.

Sally Ann Mine
Ulida Flat, Racetrack
Valley,
Death Valley.

Santa Rosa Mines
5 miles W Santa Rosa Flat
Road,
In Santa Rosa Hills.

Silver Dollar Mine
9 miles S Darwin.

Star of the West Mine
Near Trona.

Silverspoon Mine
2 miles S Trona.

Stockwell Mine
5 miles NE Valley Wells.

Surprise Mine
4 miles Ash Hill Road,
Panamint Springs.

Tee Mine
In Santa Rosa Hills.

Thorndyke Mine
9 miles S Ballarat.

Ubenheba Mine
6 miles W Lost Burro Gap.

Vega Mine
In Keynot Canyon.

White Swan Mine
5 miles E Hwy No. 190, in
Santa Rosa Hills.

Wonder Mine
7 miles Ibex Pass.

World Beater Mine
8 miles SE Ballarat.

Yaney Mine
Outside Bishop.

Kern County:

Amalia Mine
6 miles S Jawbone Well.

Apache Mine
Just outside Garlock.

Bobtail Mine
8 miles S Mohave.

Bond Buyer Mine
Outside Saltdale.

Bright Star Mine
7 miles N Claraville.

Cactus Mine
5 miles S Willow Springs.

Copper Basin Mine
Near Last Chance Well.

Digger Pine Mine
2 miles E Davis Guard
Spring.

Don Levy Mine
5 miles S Claraville.

Elephant Eagle Mine
8 miles S Mohave.

Glen Olive Mine
9 miles SE Bodfish.

Gold Bug Mine
7 miles S Ridgerest.

Gold Peak Cowboy Mine
S Loraine.

Golden Queen Mine
9 miles S Mohave.

Gwynne Mine
Near Claraville.

Hi-Peak Mine
Near Athel.

Iconoclast Mine
9 miles S Claraville.

Indian Creek Mine
2 miles SE Loraine.

Jeanette Grant Mine
10 miles S Lake Isabella.

Joe Walker Mine
2 miles Yates Hot Springs.

Laurel Mine
8 miles S Lake Isabella.

Lonely Camp Mine
4 miles S Ridgerest.

Lone Star Mine
6 miles N Claraville.

Long Tom Mine
8 miles S Granite Station.

Mohawk Buddy Mine
1 mile E Hofman Well.

Mammoth Eureka Mine
1 mile E Soda Springs.

Oakley Mine
Near Saltdale.

Opal Mine
N Saltdale.

Posomine Mine
In Pine Mts

Prospect Mine
Near Last Chance Well.

Rademacker Mine
7 miles S Ridgerest.

San Antonio Mine
Near Alpha Spring.

Seismatite Mines
N Saltdale.

Skyline Mine
6 miles S Jawbone Well.

Smith Mine
Near Garlock.

Tropico Mine
5 miles E Willow Springs.

Tungsten Chief Mine
8 miles S Havilah.

Valley View Mine
6 miles SE Bodfish.

Waterhole Mine
2 miles E Claraville.

White Rock Mine
Near Jawbone Well.

White Star Mine
6 miles S Ridgerest.

Yellow Aster Mine
3 miles Randsburg.

Zenda Mine
4 miles SW Loraine.

Lassen County:

Big Bend Mine
Big Bend, Lassen National
Forest.

Bunker Hill Mine
Big Bend, Lassen National
Forest.

Evening Star Mine
Big Bend, Lassen National
Forest.

Hornet Mine
Stoney Creek, Lassen Na-
tional Forest.

Surcease Mine
Big Bend, Lassen National
Forest.

Treasure Hill Mine
Big Bend, Lassen National
Forest.

Lost Angeles County:

Gillette Mine
In Bear Canyon.

Mono County:

Black Rock Mine
Near Benton, Casa Diablo
Mt.

Casa Diablo Mine
Near Benton, Casa Diablo
Mt.

Mono Piute Rainbow Mine
On Piute Creek,
Sacramento Canyon.

Pumice Mine
Near Benton, Casa Diablo
Mt.

Sacramento Mine
On Piute Creek,
Sacramento Canyon.

Sierra Vista Mine
5 miles S Moran Spring.

Plumas County:

Carlysie Mine
In Plumas National
Forest.

Gold Bank Mine
Near Old Forbestown,
Plumas National Forest.

Horseshow Mine
Near Junction House.

Midas Mine
In Plumas National
Forest.

Southern Cross Mine
E Coon Ravine, on S Fork
Feather River.

Walker Mine
5 miles SE Genesee.

San Bernardino County:

Amargosa Mines
SE Lake P. O.

Black Magic Mine
4 miles N Owl Springs.

Monarch Mine
4 miles N Ibex Spring,
Ibex Pass.

Morehouse Mine
3 miles N Ibex Spring,
Ibex Pass.

New Deal Mine
2 miles N Owl Hole
Spring.

Waterman Mine
4 miles N Barstow.

Shasta County:

Walker Mine
5 miles W Buckeye.

Yankee John Mine
10 miles SW Redding.

Tulare County:

Big Silver Mine
2 miles S Saltworks.

Burgess Mine
7 miles E Pine Station,
Mt. Whitney.

Ventura County:

Castac Mine
Near Buck Creek Guard
Station.

Coquina Mine
In Chino Canyon.

Frazier Mine
Near Lincoln Air Park.

Hess Mine
Near Lockwood.

Sibert Mine
Near Lincoln Air Park.

Tapo Gillibrand Mine
In Gillibrand Canyon

Yuba County:

Bootjack Mine
Near Oroville.

COLORADO

For those interested in a complete list of the early ghost towns, abandoned and lost mines of Colorado, the University of Colorado has published a volume listing nearly 300 such sites, together with their history and other background material, titled *Stampede To Timberline*, by Muriel Sibell Wolfe.

MICHIGAN

Marquette County:

Ropes Gold Mine
3 miles NE Ishpenning.

Michigan Gold Mine
2½ miles W Ishpenning.

Placer Gold Sites:

In the upper peninsula Iron Range and along the counties off the mainland bordering on Lake Michigan, numerous sites of placer gold are found from time to time. *Allegan county:* near Allegain; *Antrim county:* on Antrim River; *Charlevoix county:* on Boyne River; *Emmet County:* on Little Traverse River; *Kalkaska county:* near Walton and on Rapid River; *Leeland county:* near Lake; *Manistee county:* on Little Sable and Manistee rivers; *Montcalm county:* near

Greenville and Howard City; *Newaygo county:* on Muske-
gon River; *Oceana county:* near Whitehall and on White
River; *Ottawa county:* near Grand Haven; *St. Joseph county:*
near Marcellus and Burr Oak; *Wexford county:* near West
Summit.

MONTANA *

Beaverhead County:

Alder Gulch Placer Mines
Alder Creek.

Bannack Diggings
Grasshopper Creek, near
Bannack.

NEVADA

Churchill County:

Fairview Silver Mine
Near Fallon.

La Plata Mine
Near Stillwater.

Wonder Mine
Near Fallon.

Clark County:

Barefoot Mine
8 miles W Goodsprings.

Bullion Mine
5 miles S Goodsprings.

Cottonwood Mine
7 miles E Blue Diamond.

Crescent Turquoise Mine
Near Searchlight.

Double-Up Mine
7 miles N Goodsprings.

Golden Empire Mine
5 miles SW Nelson.

Green Monster Mine
8 miles N Sandy Hill.

---

* "Professional" ghost town for tourists in Montana's New Bannack State Park.

Key West Mine
16 miles NE "The Narrows," Lake Mead.

Lincoln Mine
6 miles S Goodsprings.

Lead King Mine
3 miles NE Dike Siding.

Lucky Jew Mine
8 miles S Goodsprings.

Milford Mine
2 miles W Well,
California.

Monte Cristo Mine
5 miles S Goodsprings.

Patsy Silver Mine
3 miles W Nelson.

Potosi Mine
6 miles SW Mountain
Springs.

Red Cloud Mine
5 miles NW Goodsprings.

Robbins Mine
9 miles N. Goodsprings.

Sultan Mine
8 miles SW Goodsprings.

Xmas Mine
11 miles SW Jean.

Yellow Horse Mine
5 miles W Goodsprings.

Yellow Pine Mine
3 miles W Goodsprings.

Elko County:

Blue Jacket Mine
Near Duckwater.

Bullion City Mine
Near Elko.

Edgemont Gold Mine
Near Elko.

Gold Creek Mine
Near Elko.

Grouse Creek Gold Mine
On Boulder Creek, NW
Shoshone Indian Reservation.

Sprucemont Mine
Near Wells.

Esmeralda County:

Black Horse Mine
12 miles W Coaldale.

Drinkwater Mine
10 miles NW Silver Peak.

Fowler Mine
7 miles W Fish Lake
Maintainance Station, on
Indian Creek.

Garnet King Mine
5 miles SW Pigeon Camp
Ruins.

Gilbert Gold Mine
Near Tonopah.

Goldsmith Gold Mine
7 miles S Tonopah.

Klondyke Mine
9 miles S Tonopah.

Micro Metal Mine
Columbus Salt Marsh,
6 miles off Hwy No. 6.

Mohave Gold Mine
12 miles S Dyer P.O.

Mohawk Gold Mine
8 miles S Dyer P.O.

Montezuma Mine
8 miles W Goldfield.

Oro Monte Mine
11 miles NW Silver Peak.

Oriental Mine
7 miles S Tule Canyon
River,
Palmetto Mt.

Palmetto Mine
Noar Lida.

Phillipsburg Gold Mine
Near Goldfield.

Piñon Mine
14 Miles W Coaldale.

Red Rock Mine
7 miles NW Fish Lake
Maintenance Station.

Roosevelt Mine
5 miles S Tule Canyon
Road, in Palmetto Mts.

Silver Moon Gold Mine
6 miles S Gold Point.

Sylvania Silver Mine
5 miles SW Palmetto, in
Palmetto Mts.

Weepah Mine
Near Tonopah.

Wiley Green Mine
12 miles S Gold Point.

Eureka County:

Buckhorn Mine
Near Beowawe.

Mineral Hill Silver Mine
Near Mineral Hill.

Richmond Mine
On Ruby Hill.

Tenabo Silver Mine
On Battle Mt.

Humboldt County:

Bolivia Mine
Outside Winnemucca.

Getchell Mine
NE Golconda.

Golden Jacket Mines
Near Mill City.

Pueblo Mine
Near Mill City.

Lander County:

Bannock Gold Mine
On Battle Mt.

Betty O'Neal Mine
On Battle Mt.

Canon City Mine
10 miles NW Kingston,
near Austin.

Clifton Silver Mine
Near Austin.

Copper Basin Mine
On Battle Mt.

Cortéz Gold Mine
On Battle Mt.

Dean Gold Mine
On Battle Mt.

Geneva Mine
Near Austin.

Guadalajara Gold Mine
Near Austin.

Kingston Gold Mine
Near Austin.

Lewis Gold Mine
On Battle Mt.

Pittsburg Mine
On Battle Mt.

Yankee Blade Silver Mine
Near Austin.

Lincoln County:

Bristol Silver Mine
Near Pioche.

Bullionville Mine
Near Pioche.

Caselton Mine
Near Pioche.

Comet Mine
8 miles W Pioche.

Frieburg Mines
Outside Hiko.

Groom Mine
35 miles SW Crystal Springs.

Ida May Mine
6 miles E Bristol Wells.

Juka Gold Mine
Near Tybo.

Jackrabbit Mine
4 miles SE Bristol Wells.

Lincoln Mine
2 miles S Tem Piute.

Lucky Star Mine
5 miles E Bristol Wells.

Old Potosi Mine
Near Mountain Springs.

Pan American Mine
9 miles SW Pioche.

Roset Mine
11 miles NW Crystal Springs.

Silver Stallion Gold Mine
12 miles NE Wilson Creek Mt.

Southpoint Mine
17 miles NW Crystal Springs.

Tem Piute Mine
9 miles S Tem Piute, near Tybo.

Woodbutcher Mine
6 miles S Bristol Wells.

Lyon-Douglas County Line:

Buckson Mine
Near Wabuska.

Lyon County:

Como Gold Mine
Near Dayton.

Ramsey Gold Mine
Near Virginia City.

Mineral County:

Granite Gold Mine
In Lodi Hills.

Pinegrove Gold Mine
Near Yerington.

Rockland Gold Mine
Near Yerington.

Nye County:

Atwood Mine
Near Luning.

Bullmoose Silver Mine
12 miles SE Beatty.

Cascade Gold Mine
8 miles E Eden Creek
Ranch.

Clay Mine
10 miles NE Beatty.

Clifford Mine
Near Tonopah.

Downeyville Mine
Near Gabbs.

Ellsworth Gold Mine
Near Ione.

Flurspor Silver Mine
6 miles E Beatty.

Goldyke Mine
Near Luning.

Hotcreek Gold Mine
Near Tybo.

Jefferson Mine
Near Tybo.

Johnnie Gold Mine
4 miles NE Johnnie.

Kawick Gold Mine
Near Tonopah.
King Tonopah Gold Mine
3 miles N Tonopah.

Lodi Mine
Near Downeyville.

Mayflower Mine
4 miles SW Springdale.

Morey Silver Mine
Near Tonopah.

Northumberland Silver
Mine
Near Belmont.

Ophir City Silver Mine
Near Austin.

Oswald Mine
7 miles E Reed.

Pioneer Mine
Near Springdale.

Pueblo Gold Mine
Near Austin.

Quartz Mountain Mine
Near Gabbs.

Reveille Mines
12 miles NE Eden Creek
Ranch, Tybo.

Royston Silver Mine
Near Tonopah.

San Antonio Silver Mine
Near Tonopah.

Silver Bow Mine
Near Tonopah.

Tonopah King Mine
3 miles NE Tonopah.

Troy Gold Mine
Near Tybo.

Wahmomie Mine
Near Beatty.

Washington Silver Mine
Near Austin.

Pershing County:

American Canyon Mine
Near Unionville.

Arabia Mine
Near Oreana.

Dun Glen Chinese Mine
Near Mill City.

Goldbanks Gold Mine
Near Winnemucca.

Rabbithole Gold Mine
Near Gerlach.

Rochester Silver Mine
Near Lovelock.

Rye Patch Silver Mine
Near Lovelock.

Seven Troughs Gold Mine
Near Lovelock

Storey County:

Gold Hill Mine
Near Virginia City.

Washoe County:

Leadville Mine
Near Gerlach.

Olinghouse Mine
Near Wadsworth.

Poe City Mine
Near Reno.

White Pine County:

Almeda Mine
Near Eureka.

Aurum Silver Mine
20 miles SE Schellbourne.

Eberhardt Mine
Near Ely.

Joy Gold Mine
Near Eureka.

Mineral City Gold Mine
Near Ely.

Newark Hill Silver Mine
Near Eureka,

Pancake Mine
Near Hamilton.

Paymaster Mine
S Mineral City.

Taylor Mine
Near Ely.

Ward Gold Mine
Near Ely.

NEW MEXICO

Beralillo County:

Ferro Mine
On Canoncito Indian Res-
ervation.

Dona Ana County:

Mountain Chief Mine
12 miles E Organ.

Stephenson-Bennett Mine
15 miles E Las Cruces, in
Organ Mts.

Grant County:

Alhambra Silver Mine
15 miles SE Silver City,
in Burro Mts.

Black Hawk Silver Mine
15 miles SE Silver City,
in Burro Mts.

Georgetown Silver Mine
9 miles NE Santa Rita, in
Mimbres Valley.

J. W. Carter Turquoise
Mine
5 miles SE Silver City, in
Burro Mts.

Naiad Queen Silver Mine
9 miles E Silver City, in
Mimbres Valley.

Piños Silver Mine
7 miles E Silver City,
2 miles N Bayard.

Rose Silver Mine
15 miles SE Silver City, in
Burro Mts.

Silver Bell Mine
9 miles NE Santa Rita, in
Mimbres Valley.

Silver Cell Mine
2 miles SE Piños Altos.

Hidalgo County:

American Silver Mine
8 miles SW Hachita.

Apache Silver Mine
12 miles SE Hachita.

Bee Hive Silver Mine
SE Hachita, at foot of
Hacjet Mt.

Gold Hill Silver Mine
12 miles NE Lordsburg.

Hachita Turquoise Mine
6 miles SW Hachita.

Jack Doyle Silver Mine
SE Hachita, at foot of
Little Hatchet Mt.

Lady Franklin Silver Mine
8 miles SW Hachita.

Leidendorf Silver Mine
14 miles S Lordsburg,
in Pyramid Mts.

Paradise Gold Mine
12 miles W Rodeo, near
Chiricahua Peak.

Prize Silver Mine
8 miles SW Hachita.

Steins Pass Mine
17 miles SW Lordsburg,
in Chiricahua Mts.

McKinley County:

St. Michael Mine
Near St. Michael.

Sandoval County:

Luciani Mines
4 miles La Ventana.

San Miguel County:

Sarah Ellen Mine
12 miles Egnar.

Santa Fe County:

Cunningham Gold Mine
10 miles E Golden, in
Cunningham Gulch, at
base of Ortiz Mts.

Shoshone Gold Mine
10 miles SE Golden, at
base of San Pedro Mts.

Sierra County:

Las Animas Gold Placer
Mines
N Hillsboro, near old
Slapjack Hill.

Taos County:

Jay-hawk Silver Mine
3 miles SE Piños Altos.

Valencia County:

Mirable Mine
Near Bluewater.

OKLAHOMA

Okfuskee County:

Devil's Half Acre Mine
8 miles S Okemah.

UTAH

Cachelo County:

La Plata Silver Mine
Near Ogden.

Beaver County:

Horn Silver Mine
48 miles W Milford.

Newhouse Silver Mine
Near Milford.

Juab County:

Diamond City Silver Mine
Near Eureka.

Emma Silver Mine
28 miles Salt Lake City,
slope Little Cottonwood
Canyon, in Wasatch Mts.

Eureka Silver Mine
32 miles Salt Lake City, E
slope Wasatch Mts.

Knightsville Silver Mine
Near Eureka.

Ontario Silver Mine
32 miles Salt Lake City, E
slope Wasatch Mts.

Silver City Silver Mine
Near Eureka.

Sunbeam Lode Mine
SW Eureka.

Salt Lake County:

Alta Silver Mine
Near Salt Lake City.

Tooele County:

Sparrow Hawk Mine
28 miles N American Fork,
in Manning Canyon,
Oquirrh Mts.

Last Chance Mine
28 miles N American Fork,
in Manning Canyon,
Oquirrh Mts.

Marion Mine
28 miles N American Fork,
in Manning Canyon,
Oquirrh Mts.

Mercur Silver Mine
On American Fork River,
in Manning Canyon,
Oquirrh Mts.

WYOMING

Fremont County:

Carissa Lode Mine
12 miles NE South Pass
City, on Willow Creek.

Federal Rules

and Regulations Pertaining

to Buried Treasure

PRESCRIBED BY the Secretaries of the Interior, Agriculture, and War to carry out the provisions of the Act for the Preservation of American Antiquities, approved June 8, 1906 (43 STAT. L. 225):

1. Jurisdiction over ruins, archeological sites, historic and prehistoric monuments and structures, objects of antiquity, historic landmarks, and other objects of historic or scientific interest, shall be exercised under the respective Departments as follows:

By the Secretary of Agriculture over lands within the exterior limits of forest reserves, by the Secretary of War over lands within the exterior limits of military reservations, by the Secretary of the Interior over all other lands owned or controlled by the Government of the United States, provided the Secretary of the Interior in the supervision of such monuments and objects covered by the act of June

FELL'S COMPLETE GUIDE

8, 1906, as may be located on land near or adjacent to forest reserves and military reservations, respectively.

2. No permit for the removal of any ancient monument or structure which can be permanently preserved under the control of the United States in situ, and remain an object of interest, shall be granted.

3. Permits for the examination of ruins, the excavation of archeological sites, and the gathering of objects of antiquity will be granted, by the respective Secretaries having jurisdiction, to reputable museums, universities, colleges, or other recognized scientific or educational institutions, or to their duly authorized agents.

4. No exclusive permits shall be granted for a larger area than the applicant can reasonably be expected to explore fully and systematically within the time limit named in the permit.

5. Each application for a permit should be filed with the Secretary having jurisdiction, and must be accompanied by a definite outline of the proposed work, indicating the name of the instituton making the request, the date proposed for beginning the field work, the length of time proposed to be devoted to it, and the person who will have immediate charge of the work. The application must also contain an exact statement of the character of the work, whether examination, excavation, or gathering, and the public museum in which the collections made under the permit are to be permanently preserved. The application must be accompanied by a sketch plan or description of the particular site or area to be examined, excavated, or searched, so definite that it can be located on the map with reasonable accuracy.

6. No permit will be granted for a period of more than three years, but if the work has been diligently prosecuted

under the permit, the time may be extended for proper cause upon application.

7. Failure to begin work under a permit within six months after it is granted, or failure to diligently prosecute such work after it has been begun, shall make the permit void without any order or proceeding by the Secretary having jurisdiction.

8. Applications for permits shall be referred to the Smithsonian Institution for recommendation.

9. Every permit shall be in writing and copies shall be transmitted to the Smithsonian Institution and the field officer in charge of the land involved. The permitee will be furnished with a copy of these rules and regulations.

10. At the close of each season's field work, the permittee shall report in duplicate to the Smithsonian Institution, in such form as its Secretary may prescribe, and shall prepare in duplicate a catalog of the collections and of the photographs made during the season, indicating therein such material, if any, as may be available for exchange.

11. Institutions and persons receiving permits for excavation shall, after the completion of the work, restore the lands upon which they have worked to their customary condition, to the satisfaction of the field officer in charge.

12. All permits shall be terminable at the discretion of the Secretary having jurisdiction.

13. The field officer in charge of land owned or controlled by the Government of the United States shall, from time to time, inquire and report as to the existence, on or near such lands, of ruins and archeological sites, historic or prehistoric ruins or monuments, objects of antiquity, historic landmarks, historic and prehistoric structures, and other objects of historic or scientific interest.

14. The field officer in charge may at all times examine

the permit of any person or institution claiming privileges granted in accordance with the act and these rules and regulations, and fully examine all work done under such permit.

15. All persons duly authorized by the Secretaries of Agriculture, War, and Interior may apprehend or cause to be arrested, as provided in the act of February 6, 1905 (33 Stat. L., 700), any person or persons who appropriate, excavate, injure, or destroy any historic or prehistoric ruin or monument, or any object of antiquity on lands under the supervision of the Secretaries of Agriculture, War, and Interior, respectively.

16. Any object of antiquity taken, or collection made, on lands owned or controlled by the United States, without a permit, as prescribed by the act and these rules and regulations, or there taken or made, contrary to the terms of the permit, or contrary to the act and these rules and regulations, may be seized wherever found and at any time by the proper field officer, or by any person duly authorized by the Secretary having jurisdiction, and disposed of as the Secretary shall determine, by deposit in the proper national depository or otherwise.

17. Every collection made under the authority of the act and these rules and regulations shall be preserved in the public museum designated in the permit and shall be accessible to the public. No such collection shall be removed from such public museum without the written authority of the Secretary of the Smithsonian Institution, and then only to another public museum, where it shall be accessible to the public and when any public museum, which is a depository of any collection made under the provisions of the act and these rules and regulations, shall cease to exist, every such collection in such public museum shall thereupon revert

to the national collections and be placed in the proper national depository.

The foregoing rules and regulations are hereby approved in triplicate and, under authority conferred by law on the Secretaries of the Interior, Agriculture, and War, are hereby made and established, to take effect immediately.

/s/ E. A. Hitchcock
Secretary of the Interior
/s/ James Wilson
Secretary of Agriculture
/s/ Wm. H. Taft
Secretary of War.

Epilogue

So, as these chapters af authenticated treasure shipwrecks and lost and abandoned mine sites—the *Catalog of Lost Treasure*—are slowly read to the last, so the bright scintillating thread of sunken and buried treasure slips now into our grasp.

Starting with King Solomon's Mines, we have traced the lure of treasure, with its more important resting places, and its wondrous pattern throughout the intricate web of the years. From those early days of the sixteenth century, it has led us ever westward through the blazing glory of the east to the no less wondrous west. And, for brief instances, its shimmering glint has led us back and forth across the seas and through the early settlement and exploitation of the New World, until the rivers of blood poured forth in its sacrifice dimmed even its radiant trail.

The *Catalog of Lost Treasure* is completed but our quest is first beginning. The story of *where* many of these known treasure sites rest is now done, but how many have been omitted! How many hundreds, even thousands, of these locations of riches are unrecorded!

From the beginning the lure of these treasure-bearing craft and the fabulous mines of the past, each with rich treasure waiting for the modern-day treasure-seeker, still retaining their wealth, has captivated the imagination. And to the end of time, ever will adventurers, salvors, and prospectors continue to seek these golden treasure-troves. The flotsam and jetsam may still be retrieved—vast hoards of riches amounting to many billions of dollars, from the wreck-sites of those once proud and stately galleons and frigates of the Old World, and also from those vessels of more modern times; from those seas, lakes, and river beds where it lies in its tomblike resting place; from out of the lost and abandoned mining camps and lodes which made history during their heyday—an everlasting lure to humankind.

The lure of treasure! Man longs ever for a sight of such glorious intriguing treasure; to gloat over it, handle it, to pocket it and spend it! It still beckons in its twinkling malicious mockery. Imagination, like Aladdin's lamp, will pierce the shrouding mist and reveal the dazzling scenes of glamor behind. The lure of treasure-seeking goes ever on and the hidden wealth is again stirring the hearts of humankind, gradually leading them into these fields afresh for the gleaming links which bind the age-long tale of wealth, into a fine-drawn glittering thread, with their ultra-modern salvage devices, their marine engineering gear, their electronic metal-locating equipment.

Just as Sir Walter Raleigh set out to discover the famous *El Dorado,* you too, reader, someday may find a way to retrieve some of those long-lost treasure chests, *for they are still there!* How long they will remain, no one knows!

Selected List

of Books to Aid

the Treasure Hunter

Arnold, Oren: GHOST GOLD. Famed story of Superstition
Mountain in the desert of southern Arizona and the
fabulous Lost Dutchman Mine. Detailed advice on how
to go about making a trip into this challenging maze of
canyons in search of a lost mine. Maps and photographs.
(The Naylor Co., San Antonio, Texas.)
Ashbaugh, Don: NEVADA'S TURBULENT YESTERDAY.
The story of the hundreds of Nevada mining towns
which boomed and withered during the last 100 years.
(Back Country Book Store, Tarzana, Calif.)
Bancroft, Caroline: COLORADO'S LOST GOLD MINES
AND BURIED TREASURE. Descriptive accounts of
lost gold mines and buried treasure in Colorado. 55 p.
illus. (Johnson Publishing Co., Boulder, Colo.)
Bancroft, Caroline: UNIQUE GHOST TOWNS AND
MOUNTAIN SPOTS. Descriptive accounts of twenty-

231

two ghost towns. 95 p., illus. (Johnson Publishing Co., Boulder, Colo.)

Brown, Robert L.: JEEP TRAILS TO COLORADO GHOST TOWNS. Comprehensive guide to Colorado's fabulous ghost towns and mining camps. (Back Country Book Store, Tarzana, Calif.)

Conrotto, Eugene L.: LOST DESERT BONANZAS. The known facts on more than 100 lost mines and buried treasures described during the past quarter-century. 278 p. illus. (Back County Book Store, Tarzana, Calif.)

Cooper, Gordon: TREASURE-TROVE PIRATES' GOLD. Twenty-five locations of treasure sites shown. 187 p. illus. (W. Funk Co., New York, N.Y.)

Cornelius, Temple H.: SHEEPHERDER'S GOLD. A group of fascinating stories of lost gold mines and buried treasure. (Back Country Book Store, Tarzana, Calif.)

Eberhart, Perry: TREASURE TALES OF THE ROCKIES. Descriptive accounts of lost treasure in the Rocky Mountains. 294 p. maps, illus. (Sage Books, Denver, Colo.)

Eberhart, Perry: GUIDE TO THE COLORADO GHOST TOWNS AND MINING CAMPS. illus. (Back Country Book Store, Tarzana, Calif.)

Florin, Lambert: A GUIDE TO WESTERN GHOST TOWNS. A guide to mining camps and towns. 96 p., illus. (Superior Publishing Co., Seattle, Wash.)

Fox, Theron: NEVADA TREASURE HUNTERS' GHOST TOWN GUIDE. A guide to Nevada's ghost towns and mining camps by counties and towns. 24 p. (San Jose, Calif.)

Francis, M. E.: JIM BOWIE'S LOST MINE. How Jim Bowie searched the Mexican records to prove the

Spaniards actually worked a rich mine in Texas. (The Naylor Co., San Antonio, Texas.)

Hintz, Naomi A.: BURIED TREASURE WAITS FOR YOU. Listing of buried treasure by states. 183 p. (Bobbs-Merrill Co., New York, N.Y.)

Hult, Ruby El.: LOST MINES AND TREASURES OF THE PACIFIC NORTHWEST. 257 p. illus. (Binfords & Mort, Portland, Ore.)

Hunt, Inez: GHOST TRAILS TO GHOST TOWNS. Ghost towns and mining camps of Colorado. illus. (Back Country Book Store, Tarzana, Calif.)

James, Henry: THE CURSE OF SAN ANDRES. The story of Soledad Mine, a site of lost treasure in caves in the San Andres Mountains of New Mexico. 163 p. (Pageant Press, New York, N. Y.)

Leary, Thomas Pennell: THE OAK ISLAND ENIGMA. A history and inquiry into the origin of the money pit, a buried pirate treasure. 36 p. (Omaha, Nebraska)

Lovelace, Leland: LOST MINES AND HIDDEN TREAS-URE. Authoritative, exact accounts, location of fortunes in California and Arizona buried treasures. 260 p. (The Naylor Company, San Antonio, Texas.)

Marlowe, Travis: SUPERSTITION TREASURES. Treasure book for the Lost Dutchman fans in Arizona. (Back Country Book Store, Tarzana, Calif.)

Miller, Charles Dean: THE TREASURE HUNTER'S MAN-UAL. 371 p. illus. (Karl von Mueller Publishing Co., Grand Prairie, Texas.)

Mitchell, John D.: LOST MINES & BURIED TREASURES ALONG THE OLD FRONTIER. Maps, illus. 240 p., (Desert Magazine Press, Palm Desert, Calif.)

Murbarger, Nell: GHOST OF THE GLORY TRAIL. Early-
day mining towns and mines. (Back Country Book
Store, Tarzana, Calif.)

Nesmith, Robert I.: TREASURE HUNTERS. 144 p., maps,
illus. (Fawcett Publications, Inc., New York, N. Y.)

Penfield, Thomas: DIG HERE! Descriptions of 65 lost mines
or buried treasures in Arizona, New Mexico and Texas.
196 p., illus. (The Naylor Co., San Antonio, Texas.)

Peters, Charles: CALIFORNIA GOLDEN TREASURES.
(Back Country Book Store, Tarzana, Calif.)

Poynton, Helen C.: WHERE TO SEARCH FOR BURIED
TREASURES. Unpaged. (Chicago, Ill.)

Pierce, Richard A.: LOST MINES AND BURIED TREAS-
URES OF CALIFORNIA. Fact, folklore, and fantasy
concerning 110 sites of hidden wealth. Maps, 56 p., illus.
(Berkeley, Calif.)

Raymond, R. W.: OLD MINES OF CALIFORNIA AND
NEVADA. Details of old mines in the Mother Lode.
(Back Country Book Store, Tarzana, Calif.)

Roscoe, Jesse Ed.: WESTERN TREASURES, LOST AND
FOUND. 123 p. (Frontier Book Co., Toyahvale, Texas.)

Roscoe, Jesse Ed.: THE GOLDEN CRESCENT. Detailing
sites of mining camps, ghost towns, finds, losses of the
southwest. (Back Country Book Store, Tarzana, Calif.)

Snow, Edward Rowe: TRUE TALES OF BURIED TREAS-
URE. 272 p. (Dodd, Mead & Co., New York, N. Y.)

Von Mueller, Karl: TREASURE HUNTERS ENCYCLO-
PEDIA. (Exanimo Press, Weeping Water, Nebraska)

Weight, Harold O.: LOST MINES OF OLD OREGON.
(Back Country Book Store, Tarzana, Calif.)

Weight, Harold O.: LOST MINES OF DEATH VALLEY.
80 p. illus. (Calico Press, Twenty-nine Palms, Calif.)

Weight, Harold O.: LOST MINES OF ARIZONA. 76 p. illuo. (Calico Press, Twenty-nine Palms, Calif.)

Woods, Dee: BLAZE OF GOLD: TREASURE TALES OF THE TEXAS COAST. 146 p. illus. (The Naylor Co., San Antonio, Texas).